# Performance Measurement of the Petroleum Industry

# Performance Measurement of the Petroleum Industry

## Functional Profitability and Alternatives

**Alan R. Beckenstein**
University of Virginia

**Leslie E. Grayson**
University of Virginia

**Susan H. Overholt**
R. Shriver Associates

**Timothy F. Sutherland**
R. Shriver Associates

**Lexington Books**
D.C. Heath and Company
Lexington, Massachusetts
Toronto

**Library of Congress Cataloging in Publication Data**
Main entry under title:

Performance measurement of the petroleum industry.

Includes index.
1. Petroleum industry and trade—United States.
2. Efficiency, Industrial. I. Beckenstein, Alan.
HD9564.P47      338.2'7'2820973      79-1951
ISBN 0-669-03017-1

*Copyright © 1979 by D.C. Heath and Company*

Published simultaneously in Canada

Printed in the United States of America

International Standard Book Number: 0-669-03017-1

Library of Congress Catalog Card Number: 79-1951

# Contents

# List of Figures

# List of Tables

# Preface

Measuring the performance of companies in the U.S. petroleum industry has been undertaken by several disciplines. Accountants have addressed the problem of external reporting; they developed most of the sources of data. Management control specialists have addressed the question of internal performance measures; they have contributed most of the insights about the actual operations of petroleum companies. Economists have addressed the question of the adequacy of competition; their theories have shed light on the numerous public policy debates about the industry.

This book reviews the evidence of the separate traditions of performance measurement. Since public policy analysis was our foremost concern, the contents of the book focus on defining useful answers to policy questions. Because sources of data are often developed for purposes other than measuring the vigor of competition, the noneconomic traditions of performance measurement are carefully reviewed.

Occasionally, the text draws negative conclusions about traditional measures of performance. This is not meant to be a denial of the usefulness of disciplines other than economics. Rather, it is a positive effort to circumscribe the applications of data and techniques to areas for which they are suited. By establishing a framework for evaluating the attributes of various sources of competitive information, the merits of alternative performance measures can be defined.

Part I offers an overview of our arguments. It outlines the considerations—business and economic—involved in performance measurement. The philosophy of the section is, quite simply, "different measures are appropriate for different uses." Part II examines the realities of the institutions in the petroleum industry and how they affect the quality and reliability of data that might be obtained.

Part III is a review of the economics of the industry. An attempt is made to exploit the knowledge about one industry to focus on the explicit usefulness of performance measures for testing public policy hypotheses. Since the industrial organization tradition of economics has less to say about performance measurement than about most other economic phenomena, this is the area where the book makes its greatest contributions. By combining the extensive knowledge of other academic traditions, the detailed institutional knowledge presented in part II, and the evidence from economic literature, some useful insights about the limitations of performance measures are obtained.

Part IV adds an empirical dimension to our arguments by citing an exhaustive list of sources of market price information. These data and others are employed in an analysis of the sensitivity of functional profitability measures to transfer price methods. The conclusion of this section is that the data contain too much "noise" to support a responsible measurement of performance using functional profitability measures.

Part V offers an analytical framework that summarizes the arguments made in previous chapters. The contributions of the book are not meant to be in any one discipline. Rather, the intersection of accounting, management, economic, and public policy knowledge is defined and applied.

At best, this work might provide a start for new research of an interdisciplinary nature on the important problem of performance measurement. At the very least, it presents a blueprint for analyzing the usefulness of sources of data for assessing the workability of competition in the petroleum industry.

# Acknowledgments

This study represents the efforts of individuals in the federal government, private industry, and the academic community. In the Department of Energy, the director of the Office of Financial Reporting deserves special acknowledgment for his guidance. We appreciate his assistance in analyzing the economic implications of the issues addressed in this study. Other members of the Office of Financial Reporting shared both their time and expertise throughout the development of this project.

Dr. Michael Schiff, director of the Ross Institute of Accounting at New York University, and Dr. Gordon Shillinglaw, professor of accounting at Columbia University, were instrumental in the early development of the issue of performance measurement in the energy industry. Executives of eleven integrated and three independent oil companies provided us with valuable insights.

Special thanks are due to Mr. Donald Van Doren, executive vice president of R. Shriver Associates. His guidance and support were present throughout the course of this study. Finally, Beckenstein and Grayson recognize the encouragement they received from several of their colleagues at the Colgate Darden Graduate School of Business Administration, University of Virginia.

The views expressed in this volume are those of the authors and do not necessarily reflect the views of the Department of Energy, R. Shriver Associates, or the University of Virginia.

# Part I
# Performance Measurement in Petroleum: An Overview

Measuring the performance of an industry or a firm is a large and complex task. In the petroleum industry, it is usually done in an emotionally charged environment. Some might find it strange and perhaps unobjective when probusiness and antibusiness lobbies can regularly reach different conclusions after observing the same phenomena. There is another explanation for the coexistence of these contradictory stances: each group is approaching the performance measurement task with different objectives. The task of performance measurement can mean different things depending on the objective of the analysis.

Let us consider an analogy: the Atlantic Ocean. How might we measure the performance of the Atlantic Ocean? As marine biologists, we might be interested in the quality of the marine environment for supporting ocean life. As astrophysicists, we might be interested in measuring the impact of lunar influences on ocean behavior. As environmental scientists, we might consider the erosion of beaches on the Atlantic coast or the interaction of fresh water bodies with the ocean. Geologists might be concerned with ocean depths and mineral deposits. Petroleum engineers would be interested in the drilling depths and the likelihood of petroleum deposits. Meteorologists would concern themselves with the location of key currents. Economists might measure the costs of traversing the ocean by alternative modes of transport.

In each of the areas of interest, some different aspect of performance would be deemed relevant. The same measure might be judged to perform well by some interest and at the same time be judged poorly by others. Suppose someone owned the Atlantic Ocean. One could easily predict that the uses of the ocean would change from their present ones. Also, the character of ownership would affect the nature of the changes. In the context of various forms of ownership, varying standards of performance could be established. In the context of common world ownership, the question of ocean performance is an irrelevant one to many people, other than those who study the law of the sea.

The performance of the petroleum industry has become the subject of much debate. Like the Atlantic Ocean, the industry can be and has been viewed from many perspectives. One would certainly expect different perspectives—accounting, economic, regulatory—to produce different performance measurement traditions. That has certainly been true. Much of this section is dedicated to reviewing the various perspectives. Before proceeding to that review, it is useful to consider principles for designing a data base to support the performance measurement task. After that, the most popular hypotheses about the industry are reviewed.

# 1

## The Fundamentals of Performance Measurement in Petroleum

### Principles for Designing a Performance Measurement Data Base

The obvious economic principle for designing a data base is to consider the benefits and costs of collecting and analyzing the data. The benefits derive from the uses to which the data are put. The costs depend on the availability of useful data and the amount of analysis needed to make the data interpretable. The distributions of benefits and costs explain a great deal of the behavior exhibited by collectors and suppliers of data.

An example of a source-oriented data base is one of the typical information systems established by a trade association. Such a system relies on the data received from the association's membership. The individual member typically uses the system to compare its performance with the industry average represented by the association's system. The polar case would be one in which all data were immediately available for all suppliers of information at a very low cost. The central source-oriented question is "What data are available?"

The opposite of source orientation is use orientation. Here the central question is "What data do I need?" In many cases economic data bases could be characterized in this category. The most important analysis might be a speculative one based on abstract theory. For example, how might gasoline prices differ if the industry were not vertically integrated? Answers to this question will certainly not be addressed by a source-oriented systems design. As will be demonstrated, performance measures useful to petroleum company management are often inappropriate candidates for regulatory analysis based on economic theory.

Between the extremes lie solutions in which use factors and source factors are integrated. This does not involve a simple cost-benefit tradeoff in which all data elements that contribute net benefits are collected. A more complex analysis is warranted. Benefits from individual performance measures cannot always be separated.

Depending on the uses of the system, sets of data will be shown useful. A process of hypothesis formation is necessary. The hypotheses will dictate combinations of industry measures that satisfy use-oriented needs. Source considerations can then be married to use considerations. Are the available data reasonable proxies for the use-dictated measures? If not, what analysis can be done to transform the data into a useful proxy? How much will this

3

transformation cost? Will the net benefits still be positive? If the data gathered are imperfect, will harm be done (in subsequent analysis) by certifying such data as official?

The process of hypothesis formation deserves some commentary. In the petroleum industry, extreme hypotheses are encountered regularly. Some analysts are certain of the "virtual monopoly" held by the major oil companies. Performance measures required to overthrow this null hypothesis would need to be conclusive. The oil industry lobbies are equally adamant in their belief that the industry is highly competitive and efficient. Here again, only highly conclusive evidence to the contrary could play any useful role.

Employing our Atlantic Ocean example, one could compare the anti-oil views to a statement that the ocean was constantly expanding its domain with the rising of the tides. The proindustry group would counter with an argument that this phenomenon was a necessary step to counter the forces causing the low tides. Certainly a final resolution of the arguments would not be forthcoming from a data system measuring the performance of the tides.

In this book, we reduce our potential hypotheses to reasonable proportions. While this implies value judgments, it can at least be understood that we recognize the impact of having made the judgments.

The process of hypothesis formation and testing should not be viewed as a static concept. We are not validating what we already know to be true. If that were the case, the value-cost tradeoff would be tilted toward collecting no data at all. A Bayesian perspective is a useful one here. Prior (to data analysis) hypotheses are formulated. The performance measurement system should then allow a capability for hypothesis revision, known as posterior analysis.

Planning for hypothesis revision, known as preposterior analysis, should be an integral part of the performance measurement process. If various outcomes were to be encountered after data collection, what further information would we then need? Possibly, we would want to stop collecting data. If that is the case, the potential value of the data is lowered.

The dynamism of the scientific process just described is often the most neglected characteristic in practice. The public policy questions that require answers in the energy industries are not "one-shot" inquiries to prove the validity of a long-standing position. The data that could be applied to them are not sufficiently robust to make final determinations about the extreme hypotheses on the behavior of oil companies.

After eliminating extreme hypotheses and static judgment uses, the problem of performance measurement in the petroleum industry can be tamed. Subsequent chapters demonstrate this in great detail.

## Major Hypotheses about the Industry

It is useful to elaborate some of the more common hypotheses about the energy industries. In the spirit of the previous section, many of the extreme and static arguments are dismissed in subsequent chapters. For now, it is sufficient that the hypotheses be exposited.

There has been much recent concern about the competitive activities within the individual business segments of the petroleum industry, particularly within the gasoline marketing segment. Much of the concern centers around the role of the major companies in the competitive environment. The concern centers primarily around size and vertical integration (operations within more than one segment of the industry), two features which, it has been claimed, have been used to inhibit competition. Specifically, individuals have alleged that the major oil companies' primary objective is the maintenance of stable, secure markets (noncompetitive ones); and that these objectives have been readily achieved by the majors' practice of controlling most of the crude oil and refined products within the integrated channels of the major companies, thereby inhibiting competition (from independent marketers) and damaging consumer interests.

While there may be competition among the majors, it is felt that the competition is intramural for shares of a market internally regulated by the vertically integrated majors. Furthermore, concerned critics contend that the cooperative arrangements and interdependency among dominant firms within the majors guarantee that the intramural competition for a larger share of the combination's market prevents entry by independent competitors but does not erupt into the full-fledged price cutting and arms-length bargaining that would threaten the stability of the integrated industry.[1]

Of particular concern is the state of competition in gasoline marketing, but competition in one segment cannot be viewed in isolation. The nature of competition in the crude market affects the competitive environment at the refinery level. Competition within the refining market affects competitive activity within the marketing sector. Integrated oil companies control the majority of crude and refined petroleum product supplies. These companies determine, under normal unregulated market conditions, the quantity of gasoline that goes to company-controlled stations and the quantity of gasoline that is sold to independents on the third party market.

If the supply of crude oil to integrated oil companies is reduced, the total available supply of refined petroleum products, including gasoline, will correspondingly decline. The integrated oil companies that control the supplies must allocate the reduced quantity between company-controlled stations and the third party market. When the oil embargo reduced the supply of crude oil in late 1973 and early 1974, independent gasoline marketers feared that the integrated oil companies would supply their own stations first, shutting off the independent marketers' only supply of petroleum products.

The ability to create such an impact on petroleum product marketing is a matter of concern to independent marketers, since their existence is at stake. It is also a concern to the public policy maker, because economic benefits accruing from competitive market forces may be jeopardized.

The federal government has attempted to respond to these concerns in many ways. The short-term solution to the supply problem was the establishment of federal allocation regulations, guaranteeing independent marketers a supply source. The Financial Reporting System (FRS) of the Department of Energy represents an additional vehicle concerned with this problem. One of its objectives is to provide information for long-term monitoring of competitive behavior within the petroleum industry. One suggested means for addressing the concerns noted is the development of functional statements of profitability for the refining and marketing segments of the industry. A primary objective of this book is to determine the feasibility of developing such statements. An equally important aspect is a determination of whether these functional statements, if developed, are necessary or useful in addressing the serious concerns about the competition issues cited, particularly within the refining and marketing segments.

Although the current concern is gasoline marketing, the issue of the most appropriate means for measuring economic performance and the competitive environment applies to any subsegment of the industry and to the industry as a whole. Therefore, this book goes beyond the problem of the viability of measuring profits of the gasoline marketing segment.

Other prominent hypotheses and questions are:

1. *Vertical Integration*
   a. Does vertical integration facilitate efficiency or control?
   b. What changes in integration are evident?
   c. Has vertical integration been used as a vehicle for predatory practices?
   d. Can efficiencies claimed to be associated with vertical integration be quantified?
   e. Can vertical integration be used as a market weapon? How? Has it been used as such in the past? When?
   f. Is vertical integration necessary for the continued maintenance of the U.S. petroleum industry?

2. *Diversification*
   a. How significant is the extent of control in various energy sectors?
   b. What patterns of, or trends in, diversification are evident?
   c. Are trends among firms similar?
   d. Is there any indication as to different levels of intensity of effort with respect to alternative fuel development?
   e. Does diversification effort include activities to design and develop new technologies?

3. *Size*
   a. Is rate of diversification associated with firm size, profitability, or degree of attained integration?
   b. How integrated are the reporting firms?
   c. Is size a necessary requirement for efficiency, risk reduction, or control?

    d. Has size been a factor in the ability to increase market share?

    e. Has size been used as a market weapon? How? Has it been used as such in the past? When?

    f. How important is size to peak spreading, risk spreading, research and development, advertising and image differentiation, and capital formation?

4. *Patterns of Change*

    a. Are company patterns of profitability and development parallel or diverse?

    b. Are changes associated with size or profitability?

    c. How do investment and production rates of development compare among alternative fuel sources? Among firms?

5. *Resource Development*

    a. Do capital formation problems exist within the industry? If so, what sector?

    b. How are investments financed? Why? What market forces influence these investment patterns?

    c. What market forces influence the development of new technology? Are vehicles for technology transfer available throughout the industry?

    d. Do commitments for investment in new technology differ among firms or fuel types? Are these commitments changing over time?

    e. How do investment and production rates of development compare among alternative fuel sources? Do they differ among firms? Are differences associated with firm size, profitability, or diversification?

    f. What is the relationship between exploration and development and reserve accretion?

    g. What investment-production relationships are evident regarding coal and nuclear energy?

6. *Impact of Government Regulation*

    a. What is the impact of Federal government regulations on nature of competition within particular segments of the industry?

    b. How large are the costs of Federal regulations? Economic impact of Federal regulation? Burden on industry? Burden on the taxpayer?

    c. Does federal tax policy impact differently alternative fuel sources?

    d. Should DOE be monitoring the efforts associated with the encouragement of development of marginal petroleum resources?

    e. What is the need for evaluation of federal funding of research and development, particularly as it occurs within the context of cooperative arrangements with reporting companies?

    f. What is the aggregate financial impact of the present system of entitlements and other federal energy regulations? In relation to each of these governmental initiatives, should policy analysis systematically relate the program to company size, profitability, and degree of diversification?

**The Financial Reporting System: A Department of Energy Mandate**

*Background*

The American economy relies heavily on the use of energy. Although the United States has only 6 percent of the world's population, it consumes 33 percent of the world's annual energy output.[2] Our economic and national well-being are directly linked to the stability of energy costs and supply. The importance of energy and the need for an awareness and understanding of the energy industry were highlighted in 1973 when the oil-producing nations, through some members of the Organization of Petroleum Exporting Countries (OPEC), imposed an embargo on exporting petroleum to the United States. Partially in concert with the embargo, the price of crude oil virtually quadrupled between 1971 and 1974, putting the United States' balance of payments under considerable and continuing strain.

The effects of the embargo rippled through the American economy. From basic industries such as steel and transportation to small businesses, the impact of limited (and therefore expensive) energy supplies was felt. The effects of the embargo underscored the critical role of energy in the economy. National security and economic issues resulting from insecure and increasingly expensive energy became immediately apparent and worrisome. For example, the oil import costs in 1973 were approximately $4 billion, while in 1977 the costs soared to about $31 billion. The result was a major capital drain, with the corresponding weakening of the dollar in the foreign exchange markets. The need for a better understanding of the energy industry by the federal government was clear.

The creation of the Federal Energy Administration (FEA), and later the Department of Energy (DOE), resulted from this need to better understand how the energy industry operated. Many information systems and programs have been initiated to this end. Information and expertise voluntarily provided by the industry itself, coupled with information from the DOE and other federal and state programs, have resulted in a much improved understanding of the energy industry.

*Purposes*

The Financial Reporting System (FRS), mandated by Section 205 of the Energy Organization Act, is one of the vehicles for providing information to energy policy makers. The development of the FRS is an acknowledgment of both the complexity of the energy industry and the need for data by the government for formulating and executing public policy.

The petroleum industry is a complex network of more than 300,000 firms responsible for extracting crude oil from underground reservoirs, refining it into usable products, and distributing the products to millions of consumers. The firms in the petroleum industry perform four basic functions: exploration and production, transportation, refining, and marketing.[3]

Each of these functions by itself is an immensely complex enterprise. Production involves thousands of wells with different locations and geological features, requiring complex and expensive drilling, equipping, and operating procedures. Transportation moves some 13 million barrels a day of domestic and imported crude oil to the nation's refineries and an average of 17 million barrels a day of domestic and imported refined products from refineries and ports to ultimate markets. The refining sector is a complex and capital-intensive industry that transforms the hydrocarbon mix of different crude oils into dozens of products. Marketing embraces the vast network of wholesalers (jobbers), fuel oil dealers, and retail service station operators who move finished petroleum products through a wide array of distribution channels from the refinery to the ultimate consumers.

Firms operating in the petroleum industry are of greatly varying sizes. At one extreme are the fifteen to twenty-five major integrated petroleum companies such as Exxon, Texaco, Mobil, Standard of California, and Gulf, which are heavily involved in all the sectors mentioned above. The other extreme is represented by the thousands of smaller companies whose activities are usually focused on just one of the functions cited.

The FRS represents an improved approach at a thorough understanding of this crucial and complex industry for purposes of public policy making. The FRS is a focused and streamlined data collection system. It is not intended to be a universal data base, groping to meet any and all present and future needs. Other energy data bases both within and outside the DOE will complement the information collected in the FRS.

The purpose of the FRS is to assist the federal government with monitoring the economic performance of the industry. More specifically, it is intended to facilitate:

Evaluation of the competitive nature of the energy industry

Monitoring of the development of domestic energy resources

Review of the impact of federal government policies and regulatory programs on the energy industry's behavior

The hypotheses related to these purposes were detailed in the previous section.

### The Performance Measurement Problem: A Preview of Alternative Philosophies

*External Reporting*

The objective of accounting practices for external reporting is to present as clear a picture as possible of the historical performance of a corporation. The theory of accounting was developed to facilitate consistency in practice among corporations. This consistency allows prospective investors to compare corporations in disparate industries.

The object of analysis is the corporation. Divisions and subsidiaries representing more than 10 percent of the sales or assets of the corporation are reported separately. No attempt is made to report by product line, vertical function, geographic location, or other attributes outside the purpose of financial reporting. Any other practice would be uneconomic, given the objectives.

Financial accounting practices are both source and use oriented. They allow some flexibility for corporate and industry practices. They also are constrained by the need to conform to the requirements of the auditing profession and to the regulations of the Securities and Exchange Commission (SEC).

In the petroleum industry, several financial accounting problems exist. Two problems relate to independent, nonintegrated companies. Some independents are privately owned. Therefore, they are not required to disclose their financial condition publicly. Also, if the independent is publicly owned, it will be required to disclose its data even if it reveals precisely its financial condition in one vertical segment in one geographic region. In contrast, the large major company will disclose only its total U.S. data at all vertical levels. In some businesses, no separate reporting occurs due to the 10 percent rule; yet the smaller independent competitor might be revealing a great deal about its performance. This informational asymmetry can work a hardship on some competitors.

*Management Accounting and Control*

The philosophy guiding the design of performance measurement systems for management is derived from the strategy the company is pursuing, the structure of its organization, and the reward system employed. In fact, companies often have different measures of performance for planning, control, and several functional areas.

Intercompany differences in each of the management variables would lead to differences in selecting relevant performance measures. Also, as companies change over time, their choice of performance measures might also change.

Comparing management and external reporting measures leads to several conclusions. Management data are more prospective than reporting data. "What if" questions are more relevant to a manager. The level of detail needed for management decision making is greater than that needed for external reporting. Even measures common to both uses might take on different values in different contexts. For example, replacement cost accounting methods are prevalent in many corporations, while financial accounting standards change more slowly.

*Economic Analysis*

Performance measurement in economics is mostly a use-oriented problem. Abstract concepts from economic theory form the basis for measurement. Two types of problems in economics require performance measurement: normative problems and positive (descriptive) problems.

Normative problems in the petroleum industry are often the focus of public policy. Comparing the performance of the industry to some ideal state, such as perfect competition, is the central task. Implicit in this type of analysis is an inquiry into the likely impact of changing some features of competition in the industry, either through governmental intervention or through the removal of such.

The positive problems in economics involve the construction of a model to predict future behavior under alternative scenarios. Such models employ both time series and cross-section data. By observing the behavior of various measures over time, prediction is facilitated as long as the future follows the trends of the past. Cross-section methods draw generalizations about corporate performance as a function of differences among the observed companies. For example, they offer a model for predicting what will happen to costs of a company as it increases its sales volume, as long as the growing company follows the path taken by the larger companies in the sample.

Often cross-section models are used to predict behavior over time of performance measures. This can be a dangerous practice. There is no necessary relationship between changes over time and differences among companies. Various trends can destroy the cross-sectional relationship.

The word "performance" takes on a different meaning in economics than it does in accounting. Performance constitutes one element in a dynamic system. Feedback from performance to the rest of the system, and vice versa, are important in understanding the nature of petroleum industry competition. In chapter 6 a conceptual model of the structure, conduct, and performance of the petroleum industry is exposited.

Ideally, economic performance analysis should be conducted with economic data. When economic data are not available, accounting data must be substituted. The limitations of accounting data as proxy for economic data are particularly evident with regard to profits. Accounting data systems are developed by business managers to assist with allocating resources within a corporation. Certain data are required by business managers to monitor the corporation's performance compared to the performance of other businesses and relative to standards set by top management. The total cost figure used to calculate *economic* profits includes a capital charge that economists regard as necessary to induce investment. *Accounting* profits are calculated by applying generally accepted accounting principles which do not—nor were they ever meant to—equate with economic profits. The conservative approach to recognition of revenue is one example of an accounting convention that is used in calculating accounting profits. Revenue is determined to be "the value of goods and services which a business entity transfers to the customers."[4] Other reasons why accounting profits must be used cautiously are that:

> Accounting profits are short-term records (annual and quarterly) of past results; the most relevant profit measure for economic analysis is prospective profits.

> Accounting profits are affected by the business cycle, whereas prospective profits, useful for economic analysis, are related to a different (future) phase of the cycle.

> Periodic and large investments are depreciated according to accounting conventions which do not reflect the current value of assets.

Simply, internal measures, such as profits, do not address economic performance. Profits, in conjunction with other measures and an economic framework, may provide a basis for evaluation. Providing the policy maker with data, over a sufficient time period, within the context of this framework, can result in useful information on which to base policy decisions.

*Preview of Conclusions*

In the chapters that follow, the analysis will:

1. *Review petroleum industry market structure.* The discussion will show that market structure exerts a strategic influence on pricing and on the nature of competition within the market. The structural dimensions will be related to economic performance. Included will be dimensions such as degree of concentration, barriers to entry, degree of product differentiation, and demand elasticity.

2. *Deliver evidence that an analysis of economic performance requires more than conclusions related to market structure.* The oil industry is, and has been, characterized by a high degree of governmental intervention, both at the federal and state levels. We will show the need for developing data that enable an under-

standing of the market behavior in a regulated market. Specifically, data are required that explain how the regulatory programs affect company policies toward setting prices, quality standards, and dealing with competitors.

3. *Explore performance measures.* Economic questions should be answered with economic, rather than accounting, data. This section of the study will examine performance as a multidimensional concept. The complex economics of the petroleum industry reduces the usefulness of simple performance comparisons. The industry is made up of many subsegments, each of which has different standards of performance. Performance measures not related to profits will be explored. The measures will be related to the economic framework described above.

It will be established also that:

1. *Corporate organization plays an important role in evaluating the oil industry.* Any data that are collected are a function of the structure of the corporation supplying the data. Because structures vary by company and industry subsegment, the meaning of the data will also vary. Data will only be as consistent as the structure of the companies and subsegments that supply them. Attempts to measure economic performance must take into consideration the nuances in the data—particularly financial data—resulting from different organizational structures.

2. *No single performance measure should be used in isolation to reach conclusions regarding competition and economic performance.* Because performance is a multidimensional concept, performance measures can only be clues as to how companies and whole industries are operating. They are not definitive answers. They must be examined in relation to structural and conduct measures to be meaningful, because absolute standards of performance for all industry segments do not exist, even at the margin.

3. *An understanding of the economics of vertical integration is necessary to evaluate the potential usefulness of performance data in assessing various competitive hypotheses.* Understanding the reasons for vertical integration is beneficial at two stages. First, the understanding assists by assuring that the design criteria consider the institutional features of the industry. Second, an understanding of the economics of vertical integration enables the policy maker to use data in a manner that makes the industry vertically accountable for its activities in each segment of the vertical chain.

4. *Although individual companies conduct functional profitability analyses, they are not desirable as a means to assess the economic performance of the energy industry.* Analysis that results from conducting functional profitability studies is based on allocated cost assumptions, does not recognize individual organizational differences among companies, and relies on transfer prices that cannot fairly represent the value of internal transfers. Functional profitability does not provide answers to questions regarding competitive issues. At best,

functional profitability raises *further* questions regarding why profits are different among different segments. Functional profitability cannot address the question of whether these profits are appropriate or inappropriate.

## Notes

1. "Petroleum Industry Competition Act of 1976," Report of the Committee on the Judiciary, United States Senate, June 28, 1976, p. 59.

2. U.S. Department of the Interior, *Report to the Secretary of the Interior by the Advisory Committee on Energy,* Washington, D.C., June 30, 1971, p. 1.

3. Federal Energy Administration Regulation, *Report of the Presidential Task Force,* Paul W. MacAvoy, ed., 1977, p. 1.

4. W.B. Meigs, A.N. Mosich, C.E. Johnson, *Intermediate Accounting,* Fourth Edition (New York, McGraw-Hill, 1978).

# Part II
# The Changing Energy Environment and the Need for Quality Data

The importance of the energy industry and the visibility of its role have increased dramatically in recent years. This pattern shows no sign of change for the immediate future. The industry and its players are at center stage.

Ours is an energy-intensive and energy-conscious society that consumes more energy than it can produce. Since it is also a society that has been unwilling to conserve the requisite amount for supply and demand balance, it is dependent on outside supply sources of questionable security. This situation has allowed a disproportionate amount of economic power to transfer to a small, albeit important, group of oil producers, specifically the OPEC cartel. OPEC's recognition and use of this power has completely changed the economic, social, and oil industry environment of energy-consuming countries.

The details of the 1973 oil embargo, the increasing demand for petroleum products, and the scarcity of future supplies have become common concerns of leaders and public policy makers. Two primary groups have responded to these problems: the public, particularly the government as the public's representative institution, and the oil companies—small and large, producers and transporters, refiners, and marketers. The changing environment has demanded a change of modus operandi. Both groups (government and industry) are very aware that our economic and national well-being are directly linked to the stability of energy costs and supply. Consequently, each is searching in good faith for a short-term arrangement that bypasses the difficulties at hand.

The government is responding to its responsibilities by evaluating the competitive nature of the energy industry, monitoring the development of domestic energy resources, and reviewing the impacts of federal governmental policies and regulatory programs on the energy industry's behavior. The development of the DOE is an acknowledgment of the importance of the energy industry, its complexity, and the federal government's need for industry data and performance measures for formulating and executing public policy.

The industry is responding to a new business environment that demands changes in business practice if the industry is to meet its corporate responsibility of providing the needed energy resources. The companies find themselves:

Negotiating from a position of comparative disadvantage with the powerful OPEC cartel

Negotiating with host countries to postpone expropriation of their reserves

Responding to changing administrations and the ebb and flow of public pressures and concerns

Responding to a maze of federal regulations and controls

Attempting to chart a business strategy in a very fluid environment

With similar long-term objectives, but with varying short-term purposes, both the government and industry have turned increasingly to performance measurements as a means for monitoring more closely the industry's activities and achieving better management control. The trend is positive. There is concern, however, regarding the application and interpretation of certain measures of performance.

> An effective performance measurement system is one that facilitates the management control process by which managers assure that resources are obtained and used effectively and efficiently in the accomplishment of the organization's objectives.[1]

> As a result, a performance measurement system must be designed on a company or situation-specific basis, reflecting the company's objectives, strategy, business organization, and managers.[2]

When one attempts to review the results of a performance measurement system, all aspects of the company's objectives and strategy must be fully understood. If they are not, confusion and misinterpretation will result. Simply, the results, outputs, and data resulting from a performance measurement system are a function of the structure and situation of the corporation that supplies the data. Because structures vary by company and industry subsegment, the meaning of the data will also vary. Data will only be as consistent as the structure of the companies and subsegments that supply them. Attempts by the government to use these data must take into consideration nuances in the data, particularly financial data, resulting from the different organizational structures.

Similarly, individual companies should exercise great caution in attempting to modify existing performance systems or attempting to use existing performance systems for purposes other than those which they were originally designed to serve.

The following chapter discusses these considerations in greater detail. A discussion of the organization of the petroleum companies is provided. The piece reviews the internal organization of corporations and shows what an important role they play in the evaluation of the performance of the oil industry. Next, a discussion of a specific performance measurement, functional profitability, is provided. Functional profitability is seen as a measurement tool used by corporate managers and its applicability to evaluating segments of the petroleum industry is discussed. Finally, transfer pricing and specific transfer pricing practices in the industry are discussed. The chapter shows how transfer pricing systems are often part of a company's effort to gather internal quantitative information for making decisions regarding how to use the company's resources most efficiently. The discussion reviews how oil companies are particularly sensitive to accurate data collection because they have large capital investments that must be used efficiently and narrow per unit margins in which to operate.

## Notes

1. R.N. Anthony, J. Dearden, and R. Vancil, *Management Control System, Text Cases and Reading*, (Homewood, Ill., Richard D. Irwin, Inc., 1972), p. 147.
2. Ibid.

# 2

# The Organization of Petroleum Companies

## Organizational Structure

The internal organization of corporations plays an important role in the evaluation of the economic performance of the oil industry. At first glance, the oil industry appears homogenous. In reality, it is made up of subsegments comprising companies that vary by size, product, and geographical market emphasis, as well as in other ways.[a] These variations result from each corporation's analysis of how it can compete in the economic environment. Based on the analysis, a corporation selects a corporate strategy, strategy referring to the determination of a company's basic long-term goals and objectives. Strategy also includes the adoption of courses of action and the husbanding of resources necessary to carry out these goals.[1]

A corporation selects an organizational structure to fit its strategy. Any data collection effort is influenced by the structure of the corporation supplying the data. Because structures vary by company and industry subsegment, the meaning of the data will also vary. Data will only be as consistent as the structure of the company and subsegment that supply them. Attempts to measure economic performance must take into consideration the nuances in the data—particularly financial data—resulting from the different organizational structures.

Organizational structures are made up of building blocks of business units. These business units vary in their levels of responsibility and complexity. This book focuses on functions, which can be viewed as a series of specialized activities that are process oriented. The production process at an automobile company is often thought of as the manufacturing function. The marketing function of that same company would represent the process of selling the finished product to retail automobile dealers. The same is true of the refining process of an oil company. Refining is only one of the many functions required to turn the crude oil in the ground into the gasoline that is pumped into the automobile.

Corporations vary in how they group activities to form a functional business unit. Interviews with integrated oil companies pointed out, for example, that each company defines marketing differently. In Company A, the marketing

---

[a]Subsegment or segment refers to classes of companies within the oil industry. Examples of industry subsegments include regional, national, independent, integrated, small, and large.

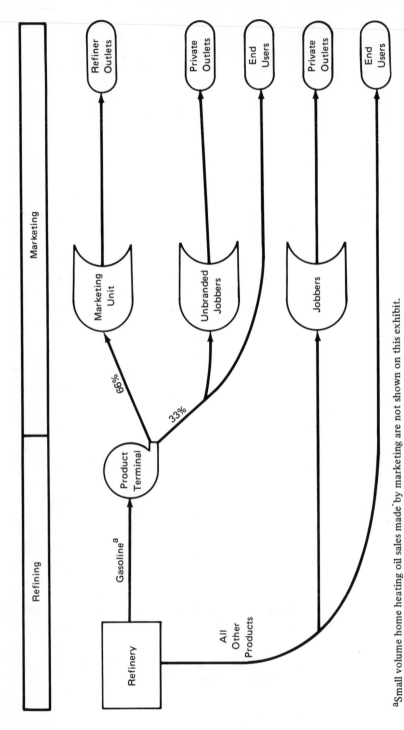

**Figure 2-1.** Company A. Product Distribution System

[a]Small volume home heating oil sales made by marketing are not shown on this exhibit.

function's primary activity is the selling of retail-branded gasoline and home heating oil. The marketing function's responsibilities begin on the outlet side of the product terminal (figure 2-1).

In contrast, Company C defines marketing as all those activities that occur on completion of the refining process. Figure 2-2 illustrates the greater responsibilities that Company C's marketing function has compared to Company A's marketing function. Specifically, the marketing function in Company C is responsible for the storage and the sale of all products, whereas the marketing function in Company A handles only the sale of retail-branded gasoline and a small volume of home heating oil. Company E offers a third form of responsibility division between refining and marketing (figure 2-3). The company has set up two marketing groups: industrial and wholesale marketing within refining; and branded jobber and retail marketing within marketing. The marketing unit assumes the costs for storing all products that it sells. These differences must be considered when designing a data collection system for performance evaluation.

Data collected on a company-wide basis are influenced by differing accounting techniques. Data collected on units within companies are additionally influenced by the structure through which each company has chosen to operate. Even if Companies A and C and E process and sell the same quantity of petroleum, and the total refining and marketing costs for each company are identical, the costs reported by Company A's marketing unit will be lower than those reported by either Company C or E. This occurs not because Company A is more efficient, but because Company A has limited the marketing function's operations to the sale of retail-branded gasoline and home heating oil. The costs of marketing all other products are borne by the refining function. The marketing units of Companies C and E have the responsibility (and corresponding expenses) for storing and selling a large number of products. Companies A, C, and E represent three alternative approaches to corporate structure. Additional organizational differences that complicate the creation of a standardized industry-wide data collection system are described in chapter 5.

The problem of which responsibilities (and costs) should be included in refining versus marketing is not new. In the first phase of the FRS, DOE defined each of these segments for reporting purposes.

> In general, refining operations should be considered as having ended when product is delivered into transportation facilities.

> Include operations of terminals, bulk plants, retail outlets, and transportation facilities used for delivering refined products in the marketing function. Include operations of canning plants (e.g., blending, compounding, and canning lube oil products) in refinery operating expenses.[2]

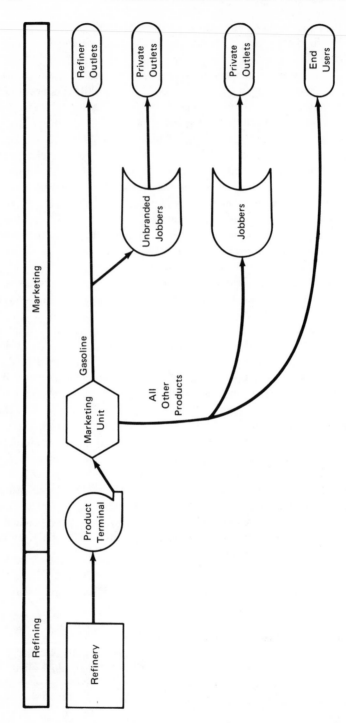

**Figure 2-2.** Company C. Product Distribution System

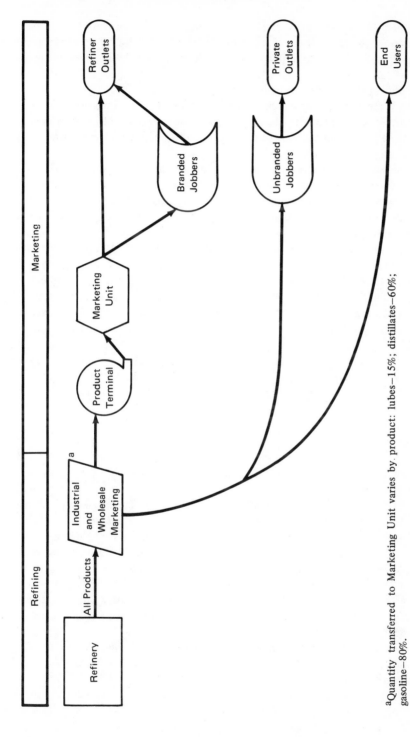

ªQuantity transferred to Marketing Unit varies by product: lubes—15%; distillates—60%; gasoline—80%.

**Figure 2-3.** Company E. Product Distribution System

These definitions follow closely the organization of Company C. However, the refining and marketing units of Companies A and E must be artificially re-arranged for DOE reporting purposes to fit them into the defined boxes (figures 2-4, 2-5, and 2-6).

Defining the business units in a prescribed manner, as the DOE chose to do in FRS-Phase 1, is one approach to comparing the operations of subsegments of an industry. Unfortunately, this approach ignores the fact that each company has selected its corporate structure to operate most effectively, according to its analysis, in the market place.

Executives assess internal strengths and weaknesses, market conditions, strengths and weaknesses of their competition, supply conditions, and other environmental factors, such as government regulations, when determining a corporation's strategy. Examples of strategic choices include: expanding volume of activities (Cities Service's marketing effort in the early 1960s); setting up distant plants and offices (Texaco's strategy to market in 50 states); moving into new economic functions (Arco's movement into the coal industry); and be-coming diversified among many lines of business (Mobil's purchase of Marcor).

Companies determine how they should be organized based on the strategy that they have decided to follow. Changes in structure follow changes in strategy. An oil company that is short of crude oil supplies will choose a different corpo-rate strategy and, therefore, a different organizational structure, from one that has been historically long on domestic crude. Transportation links, refinery capacity and location, market size, and location and diversity of product lines are other considerations that affect an oil company's choice of organizational strategy and structure.

Historically, companies have made major structural changes based on strategic actions that develop from an evaluation of changes in internal and ex-ternal factors. The struggle at the du Pont Company shortly after World War I provides a clear illustration of the types of organizational changes necessitated by altered market conditions. Prior to that time, Du Pont's growth was the result of expanding the output of its one product: explosives. The single product line business strategy was carried out by a functional organization. After World War I, the demand for explosives declined, and du Pont faced the problems of excess production capacity and low utilization of its research laboratories and sales organization. The company also needed to find customers to fill the gap left by the decline in government business. Du Pont turned to chemical-based products in its effort to diversify. The new product lines required vastly different manu-facturing processes and different marketing techniques from the old single product line. The functional organization was no longer the best framework for implementing du Pont's corporate strategy. After considerable internal turmoil, a divisionalized structure based on product lines was created to replace the func-tional organization.[3]

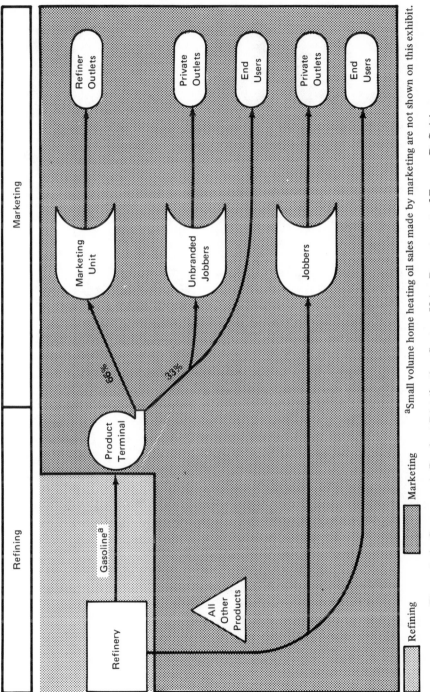

**Figure 2–4.** Company A. Product Distribution System Using Department of Energy Definitions

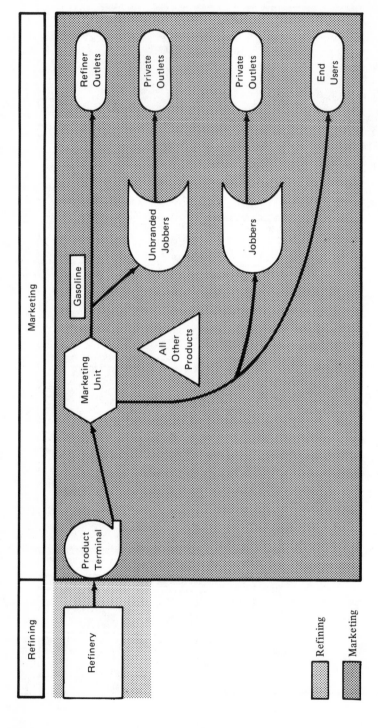

**Figure 2-5.** Company C. Product Distribution System Using Department of Energy Definitions

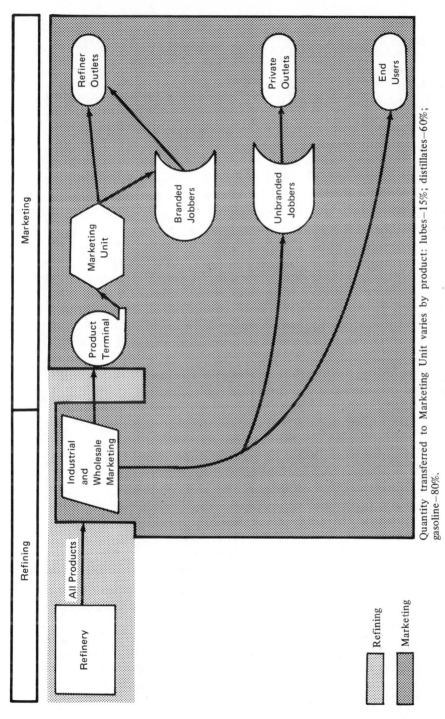

Quantity transferred to Marketing Unit varies by product: lubes—15%; distillates—60%; gasoline—80%.

**Figure 2-6.** Company E. Product Distribution System Using Department of Energy Definitions

A more recent example of structural alterations to complement strategic change is the approach that Sun Company is taking. Anticipating the company's future shortage of guaranteed crude oil supplies, Sun Company decided to establish separate subsidiaries, each bearing both manufacturing (or purchasing) and marketing responsibilities. In the past, the activities of the business units were highly integrated. Marketing sold products that the Sun refineries processed from oil produced by Sun in wells discovered by Sun employees. The structure was organized around functions representing physical tasks that move crude oil from wells through refining and marketing to the end consumer (figure 2-7).

The new structure (figure 2-8) allows areas that were formerly process oriented to make decisions about where they purchase and sell their products. The refining division can now choose whether to use Sun oil or to buy crude oil from a third party marketing company.

In making the change, the Sun Company believes that it has found a more flexible structure for responding to market factors affecting the company. Any of the divisions can be removed (through sale or dissolution) and the company remains a whole, without major disruption. If the marketing division were sold, for example, the refining division would begin to sell all of its products to third parties, rather than only a portion of them. Because a marketing department exists within the refining division, the loss of the marketing division represents the loss of a customer rather than the loss of the recipient of the refinery division's entire output.

The strategy and structural changes at Sun Company are particularly significant because they may signal the end of the company's policy of verfical integration. Vertical integration, currently the dominant structural feature of the oil industry, is discussed in greater detail in chapter 7.

Corporations continuously monitor the performance of business units. The methods used for evaluation vary, but the major one of interest to us here is functional profitability, which is discussed in the next chapter.

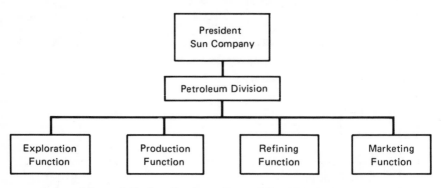

**Figure 2-7.** Sun Company Prior to Structural Change

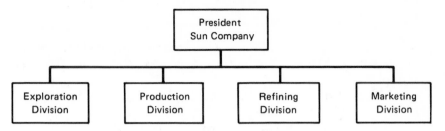

**Figure 2-8.** Sun Company's Proposed Structure

## Summary

Understanding the differences in corporate structure is important for two reasons. First, any data collected by the federal government to measure the economic performance of the industry are influenced by the structure of the corporation that supplies them. Second, a corporation's structure reflects the industry's own continuous analysis and conclusions regarding market conditions and competition.

An endogenous process operates continuously. Profits and other favorable aspects of performance invite entry or expansion, or both of member firms. As the economics of the industry (and its subsegments) change, so also will there be changes in the strategies and structures of the corporations as they pursue their share of the profits. These adaptations lead to changes in the organizational performance incentives.

This inevitable cycle of competition, complex as it may be, is the background against which performance must be measured. The information available from corporations is influenced by this overall competitive process. It is influenced also by institutional nuances, differences in objectives, and judgmental errors. The gaps in the marketplace left by integrated majors will be filled by independents whose raison d'être is entirely different. Therefore, the objectives and structures of classes of oil companies must be considered in evaluating performance.

Understanding why companies organize differently is a prerequisite for determining if their performance is appropriate. By redefining the structures so they are standardized, one loses the significance of the differences and may even camouflage the effects of a basic industry characteristic, such as vertical integration, that should be analyzed. The impact of molding disparate corporate organizations into one form depends on the significance of the use of the data that will be generated based on the artificial structure. The development of profit and loss statements based on artificial structures is more sensitive, for example, than development of costs, because more variables are involved.

## Notes

1. A. du Pont Chandler, Jr., *Strategy and Structure, Chapters in the History of the Industrial Enterprise,* 2nd printing (Cambridge, Mass., The MIT Press, 1963), pp. 78–88.

2. *Federal Register,* volume 43, no. 121, Thursday, June 22, 1978, p. 27128.

3. Chandler, *Strategy and Structure,* pp. 112–113.

# 3

## Functional Profitability and the Need for Transfer Pricing

The appropriate tools required to conduct performance evaluation vary depending on the purposes of the assessment. Three distinct points of view characterize the corporate manager who is making decisions about allocating corporate resources; the outside investor who must decide in which company and in which industry to place an investment; and the policy maker who must determine what (if any) government action should be taken to influence industry behavior.

In some cases, the public policy maker will find that internal management and outside investor performance measures provide meaningful information for making decisions. In other cases, measures commonly used by internal corporate management or outside investors are inappropriate for public policy analysis. The measures may provide no information for addressing the issues of competition, resource development, and impact of policy, or may lead the public policy maker to incorrect conclusions.

This chapter discusses functional profitability, a measurement tool used by corporate managers, and its applicability to evaluating segments of the petroleum industry. Developing profit and loss statements by functions (refining and marketing) of integrated companies would allow analysts to compare the profits of segments of integrated oil companies with the profits of independent refiners and marketers.

### Profits and Their Measurement

Profits are the difference between sales revenue and total costs incurred to earn the revenue. Measures of profitability are intended to indicate how effective corporate or business unit policies and decisions were in generating profits.

An industry's (or corporation's) profits form the foundation for new investments and industry (or corporate) growth. They must also be used for rewarding, in the form of dividends, the investors who have committed resources to the industry (or corporation). As such, they are an important indicator of the economic performance of both an industry and a corporation.

Profits as defined here are the same as the net income figure reported to stockholders. The calculation of profits on a functional basis requires decisions by management regarding what should be included in the total costs portion of the profit equation for each function.

Recognition of profits yields some obvious intricacies. High reported profits could be caused by high revenues from market power, low costs, or a combination of both. Likewise, low reported profits could be caused by low revenues due to strong competition, high costs due to poor efficiency, or a combination of both. Likewise, low reported profits could be caused by low revenues due to strong competition, high costs due to poor efficiency, or a combination of both. High profits may be required to justify high-risk investments. Research by economists has long been plagued by the inadequacy of data for testing economic hypotheses, such as the relationship between industry concentration and profitability.

Many performance measures based on profits are used by internal corporate managers and outside investors. Cash flow and return on investment are two such measures.

*Cash flow* refers to the money generated by one or more business units. There is no one equation for calculating cash flow. One common equation for corporate-wide cash flow analysis is: cash flow = profits after tax + depreciation (a noncash expense). Cash flow is a useful measure for estimating if a business unit is contributing to or extracting from the overall profits of a corporation. On a corporate or industry basis, cash flow is a measure of the dollars that the total corporation or industry generates for future investments in energy resource development or in other areas.

*Return on investment* (ROI) has become a classical performance measure tool, used by internal corporate managers, outside investors and public policy makers. To calculate an ROI, the corporate manager is concerned with the relationships of all the factors that make up both the return (profits) and the investment base. The final return on investment is equal to the profits, however they are defined, divided by the investment base, however inclusive it may be. The formula is: ROI = profits ÷ investment required to earn the profits.

Like any ratio, the ROI is very sensitive to changes in the numerator and denominator. Given the same dollar profits, the ROI can change significantly by including a different collection of assets in the investment base, such as gross instead of net fixed assets, or portions of current assets deducting current liabilities. Likewise, a change in the method of calculating profits can alter the ROI, even though the investment base remains constant. Nevertheless, if definitions are kept constant from one accounting period to another, ROI can be useful to compare the changes in performance of a company or industry.

## Calculation of Functional Profitability

*Theory and Practice of Transfer Pricing*

Many performance measures can be calculated for individual business units without regard to the interaction between units. These include actual costs compared to budgeted costs, and actual sales (both volume and value) compared to forecast sales. Other measures focus on the interaction of business units in a company. These measures require that both costs and revenues of a business unit be determined. Profitability measures such as profits before tax, profits after tax, and ROI are three such examples.

Sales revenues are not recognized by accountants until the title of the product has passed to a third party. Therefore, the transfer of goods from one business unit to another within the same company is considered to be a change in the location of inventory and not a sale.

To evaluate the refining and marketing functions of companies in the oil industry on the basis of profits, a value must be assigned to each unit of product as it moves from the refining function to the marketing function. That value, which is a unique price developed for internal sales (transfers), is called a *transfer price.*

Through the use of transfer pricing, values are assigned to all of the products that are passed from the refining function to the marketing function. The sum of these values serves as both the revenues for the refining function and the product costs for the marketing function when profitability calculations are made.

Transfer prices represent a connecting link between two business units. They supply information for decision making and serve as a tool to evaluate a business unit's financial performance. Transfer pricing systems have been developed for two main purposes: management control and resource allocation.

**Management Control.** Transfer prices serve two primary functions in the area of management control: to ensure goal congruence and to measure the performance of business units.

*Goal Congruence.* In a small organization, the owners can personally encourage all parts of the organization to work together to meet the common goal for which the organization was formed. As organizations grow, however, formal means of ensuring goal congruence are required. As personal control becomes infeasible because of the size of the organization, management control systems are established to motivate people to make managerial decisions that are in the best interests of the corporation as a whole. Transfer pricing may be part of the control system.

For example, when gasoline is processed by ABC Oil Company's refinery, coke is created as a by-product. Because the volume of coke sales will be small compared to other major products, and coke has a narrow profit margin, the marketing unit normally would not choose to expend any effort selling the product. To encourage the marketing unit to sell the product, ABC Oil Company establishes a price for the transfer of coke from refining to marketing. A low price will give marketing a large profit margin and make sales attractive. The refineries can, therefore, be assured of an outlet for a product they create in the process of making gasoline. In addition, corporate resources are not invested in large inventories of unsold coke. The transfer price encourages the business units to work together toward a common corporate goal.

*Business Unit Performance Evaluation.* Transfer pricing can also assist management with measuring the performance of individual business units. Because each business unit has a certain role or set of responsibilities in the corporate structure, it can be considered a responsibility center. There are two major types of responsibility centers: cost and profit.

Top management will evaluate the performance of the business unit that is a cost center on the basis of actual costs compared to forecast costs. The performance evaluation of a profit center focuses on the business unit's revenues compared to the costs incurred to earn those revenues. Depending on a company's corporate strategy and the corporate structure created to carry out the strategy, business units will be set up either as cost or profit centers.

When products are transferred from one business unit to another within a corporation, a transfer price serves as the link that allows profit analysis. One corporation may consider refining and marketing as two separate functions, each of which is evaluated as a cost center. Actual information is gathered for each business unit and compared to the expected costs. The performance of the units is evaluated accordingly.

Another corporation, with a different corporate stragegy, may decide that the function of refining should be a cost center, but that the marketing function should be a profit center. The refining function would be evaluated the same as in the previous example. However, new information is required to evaluate marketing as a profit center. Product costs as well as operating costs must be collected. If marketing had purchased its product from a third party refinery, the costs would be readily available from the purchasing department. But, if the product is transferred from a refinery within the corporation, a unit value (the transfer price) for the product must be determined before performance evaluation can be made. Specific methods that can be used will be discussed later. The information may be used to determine if the value received from the business unit justifies the resources spent on it.

Decisions that might result from such analysis include: buying crude oil from a supplier rather than owning and operating an internal production function; selling petroleum products from refineries to independent marketers rather than selling them through the company's marketing function; and building a new refinery because the refining function operates more efficiently and can supply petroleum products more cheaply than an outside supplier.

**Resource Allocation.** Transfer prices serve three purposes in the area of resource allocation: to assist with capital budgeting decisions, to allocate taxes, and to optimize corporate activities.

*Capital Budgeting.* Capital budgeting decisions (planning expenditures whose returns are expected to extend beyond one year) represent the most important series of decisions that a company makes. These decisions are critical to the future well-being of the firm. They should result in the firm having the proper mix and quantity of assets at the right time, so that it can compete effectively in the market. Every business unit—production, refining, transportation, and marketing—is affected by the capital budgeting decision. As a result, managers of business units want to ensure that the most credible information reaches top management. To do so, revenues and costs associated with particular projects must be estimated for the life of the project. This often requires the use of a transfer pricing system.

For example, ABC Oil Company is considering building a new refinery, which will be used for fifty years. The refining unit manager needs to determine the costs that will be incurred and the revenues that will be received if the refinery is to be built. Costs can be estimated based on historical information and budget projections. Since all of the output of the new refinery will be transferred to the marketing unit and not sold to a third party, the manager has no revenue data to relate to the cost data. A transfer price is required to estimate the revenues attributable to the product as it moves from the new refinery to the marketing unit.

*Tax Allocation.* Corporations are subject to taxes imposed by state and federal governments as well as foreign governments. To maximize after-tax earnings, corporations may use transfer prices to determine the most favorable location in which to earn profits.

For example, ABC Oil Company owns a refinery in State A that has a 10 percent corporate income tax rate. It markets gasoline in States B and C, both of which have a 15 percent corporate income tax rate. The company can calculate income taxes by the Massachusetts formula[a] or by a comparable formula. Using its own transfer pricing formula, ABC Oil Company can, for state tax purposes, sell its gasoline from the refining unit to the marketing unit at a high transfer price. This will allow the company to show higher profits in State A, in which the refinery is located, and which has the lower tax rate. The marketing unit will pay taxes on lower profits, because of the high transfer price it must pay. The corporation, therefore, will pay out less of its earnings in taxes. This same concept is also used to move profits from one country to another, to take advantage of different tax rates and to overcome foreign exchange controls.

Internal revenue regulations allow transfers that result in an overall tax savings, provided that the transfers are not made for the sole purpose of avoiding a tax liability. Two common tests are the *arm's length* test and the *business*

---

[a]Allocated on the basis of sales, property and payroll within the respective state.

*purpose* test. A transfer meets the arm's length test if the price is fair and reasonable to two unrelated parties dealing in an open market. The business purpose test can be met if the transfer serves some demonstrable, though marginal, purpose other than tax savings.[1]

When transfer pricing is used for both management control and tax allocation, managers may receive confusing signals regarding how they should perform.

In the preceding example, the marketing functions in States B and C may not appear profitable, whereas they would if a lower transfer price were used. Managers should be wary of making operating decisions based on transfer pricing systems designed for tax purposes.

*Corporate Optimization.* Transfer pricing serves one basic purpose: to meet corporate objectives by ensuring that all business units operate in the way that is best for the entire corporation. The impact that a transfer price can make on total corporate performance is illustrated in the following example.

ABC Oil Company is organized into the refining function and the marketing function. A third party handles all transportation requirements. Each business unit has the authority to purchase and to sell to the customers of its choice. The refining function sells both to independent gasoline marketers and to the marketing function. The marketing function buys from both the refining function and outside refiners. To illustrate the impact of a transfer price on corporate operations, this example focuses on one decision: Should the refining function sell the 200,000 barrels of gasoline it produced this month to an independent gasoline marketer or to the marketing function where the company's special

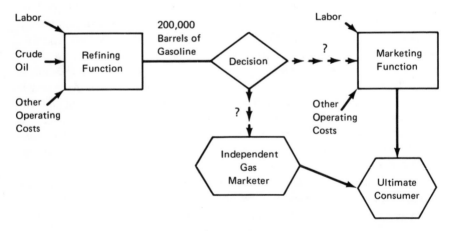

**Figure 3–1.** Corporate Optimization: Decision Regarding Third Party Sales

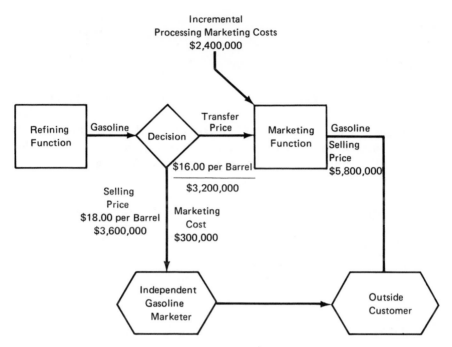

**Figure 3-2.** Corporate Optimization: Information Requirements

additive will be blended in and the product then sold through the company's own service stations (figure 3–1)?

The transfer price that is used should encourage the refining manager to make the decision that maximizes the resources of the entire corporation. The transfer price should lead business unit managers to make the same decision headquarters' managers would make if they had the time to study the problem and apply all the data available to the managers of business units.[2] Transfer prices that do not meet this standard will result in suboptimization.

If the refining function sells the gasoline to an independent marketer, the division will incur $300,000 in marketing costs. If the refining function transfers the gasoline to the marketing function, that function will spend $2,400,000 on processing and marketing activities, then receive $5,800,000 for the 200,000 barrels at the service stations. A selling price to independents has been set at $18.00 a barrel, while the transfer price to the marketing function has been set at $16.00. Figure 3–2 illustrates the information available for deciding to whom the sale should be made.

The refining function manager would base the decision on the following relevant information:

|  | Sale to Independent Gasoline Marketer | Transfer to Marketing |
|---|---|---|
| Revenues | $3,600,000 | $3,200,000 |
| Marketing Costs | 300,000 | 0 |
| Profit Contribution | $3,300,000 | $3,200,000 |

Because the division can earn $100,000 more by selling the 200,000 barrels to an independent gasoline marketer, and assuming that the division is evaluated by its level of profits, the refining manager would decide to sell the gasoline to the independent.

An individual who had responsibility for both the refining and the marketing functions and who used all the information given in figure 3-2 would reach a different conclusion. If the interests of the entire corporation are considered, the alternatives appear differently:

|  | Sale to Independent Gasoline Marketer | Sale to Ultimate Consumer Through Marketing Function |
|---|---|---|
| Revenues | $3,600,000 | $5,800,000 |
| Costs: |  |  |
| Marketing by Refining Function | 300,000 | 0 |
| Processing and Marketing by Marketing Function | 0 | 2,400,000 |
| Profit Contribution | $3,300,000 | $3,400,000 |

The corporation as a whole can earn $100,000 more by absorbing the marketing function's $2,400,000 in marketing and processing costs, not incurring $300,000 in marketing costs in the refining function, and selling the product directly to the consumer through company-owned gasoline stations.

With different processing and divisional marketing costs or different revenue levels, the optimal corporation decision could have been reversed. If the corporation is relying on the transfer price to trigger the best overall decision, the price must be determined carefully. One transfer price that will encourage the refining manager to make the correct decision and avoid suboptimization is the gasoline's opportunity cost.[b] In this instance, the transfer price would be the total expected revenues from the sale of 200,000 barrels of gasoline to the independent

[b]Opportunity cost of using a resource for a specified purpose is the net present value of the cash flow it would generate in its best alternative use. Figures used here are for illustrative purposes only.

gasoline marketer ($3,600,000) minus the associated marketing costs ($300,000) not incurred by refining because the gasoline is transferred to marketing, all divided by the number of barrels involved in the transaction, as follows:

$$\frac{\$3,600,000 - \$300,000}{200,000 \text{ barrels}} = \$16.50/\text{Barrel}$$

This price of $16.50 a barrel makes the sale to the independent marketer no more profitable (to the refining function) than the transfer to the marketing function. Using this transfer price, the refining function manager will choose to transfer the gasoline to the marketing function.

|  | Sale to Independent Gasoline Marketers | Transfer to Marketing Function |
|---|---|---|
| Revenues | $3,600,000 | $3,300,000 |
| Costs: | | |
| Marketing by Refining | 300,000 | 0 |
| Profit Contribution | $3,300,000 | $3,300,000 |

**Notes**

1. National Industrial Conference Board.
2. Gordon Shillinglaw, *Managerial Cost Accounting,* fourth edition, (Homewood, Ill., Irwin Press, 1977,) p. 848.

# 4

# Transfer Pricing: The Basic Problem

## Methods of Calculating Transfer Prices

When a company decides to use a transfer pricing system, whether for management control or resource allocation, it needs a basis for calculating individual transfer prices (the unit value of a product as it moves from one business unit to another). Several methods have been developed to calculate transfer prices. Each of these methods is discussed here.

Regardless of what method is used, three sets of activities occur (figure 4-1). First, a transfer price is determined based on one of the methods described here. The price may be determined by an accountant, who calculates the standard cost of a product; a manager, who monitors the market price; or an economist, who calculates the marginal cost.

Second, based on the transfer price, a decision is made. For example, a marketing manager might see that the transfer price is lower than the price required to purchase the product on the outside market. As a result, the manager may choose to acquire all of the marketing unit's petroleum products from the company's refining unit.

Finally, the results of the decision are evaluated. With transfer pricing, top management has the capability to quantify both costs and revenues for each business unit and may, for example, elect to evaluate the profit performance of the market unit at the end of the fiscal period.

Each set of activities contains a range of possible actions, including who determines the transfer price and how it is determined; who decides on a course of action and how that decision is made; and what results are evaluated.

The six basic transfer pricing methods discussed here include cost-based, marginal cost, two-step approach, market-based, negotiation, and linear programming. For illustrative purposes, refining and marketing units are the relevant business units of all examples in this section.

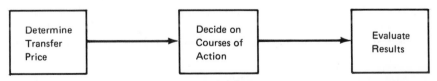

**Figure 4-1.** Transfer Pricing: Activities

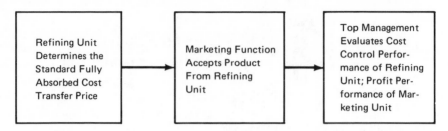

**Figure 4–2.** Cost-Based Transfer Price in Functional Organization

## *Cost-Based*

The first transfer price method developed was based on cost. Pinning the transfer price of a product to its cost reflects the concept that transfers are only a change in the location of corporate inventory. There are many different kinds of transfer pricing arrangements based on cost. The most widely used is standard fully absorbed cost[a] which is discussed here. Other variations, including actual costs and cost-plus, are sufficiently similar that a separate discussion is not necessary.

The standard fully absorbed cost of a product is determined by appropriate personnel in the refining unit. If the marketing unit is allowed to make purchasing decisions, a manager will then decide whether to purchase the product from the refining unit at the transfer price or to buy the product from an outside supplier.

In a vertically integrated company, the marketing unit is probably a function that does not have purchasing authority and must accept the product at the transfer price (figure 4–2).

At the end of an accounting period, top management evaluates the performance of both the refining and marketing units. The performance evaluation of the refining unit is based on cost control; the performance evaluation of the marketing unit is based on profitability. Only the marketing unit is a profit center when the cost-based method is used; the refining unit remains a cost center.

The cost-based method is the easiest one to implement because it relies on standard cost data that are usually developed for accounting purposes. However, there are several problems with implementing a transfer pricing system based on costs. First, the method does not take into consideration the fact that the refining unit has fixed costs that will be incurred regardless of the quantity of goods that are transferred to the marketing unit. Although the cost of the product that refining produces is variable from the marketing unit's viewpoint,

---

[a]Standard fully absorbed cost is the predetermined cost including material, labor, and all factory overhead (fixed and variable), at a specific output level.

if marketing can choose whether or not to buy, the cost to the corporation is partially fixed and partially variable. The marketing unit may decide not to buy based on a cost-based transfer price because the price is higher than one quoted by an outside supplier. If the refining unit must incur inventory or selling costs as a result, or fails to cover its fixed costs, the decision not to buy from the refining unit is not in the best interests of the entire corporation.

The following example (figure 4–3) illustrates the danger of suboptimization caused by using the cost-based method to determine a transfer price.

The marketing manager for the ABC Oil Company must decide whether to purchase residual fuel requirements from an outside vendor or from the company's refining unit. The outside supplier's price is $10 per barrel and the internal cost-based transfer price is $12 per barrel. With only that information and given that the marketing unit is evaluated on profit performance, the marketing manager would choose to purchase the product from the outside supplier.

However, the refineries are operating below capacity, and the opportunity cost of internal transfers is the average variable cost of $9, not the $12 full cost. Therefore, if the product is purchased outside, the refining unit will lose a $3 contribution toward its fixed costs; the loss in total company profit will be $1 per barrel ($10–9=$1).[1]

Because of the danger of arriving at suboptimal decisions using fully absorbed standard costs as a transfer price, corporations often decide either to require that the marketing unit buy from the refining unit if capacity is available

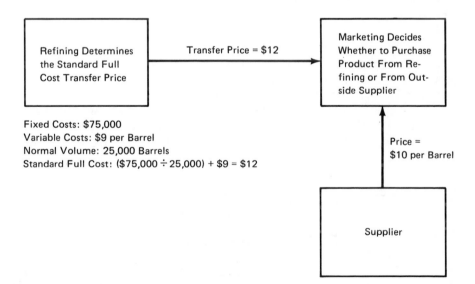

Fixed Costs: $75,000
Variable Costs: $9 per Barrel
Normal Volume: 25,000 Barrels
Standard Full Cost: ($75,000 ÷ 25,000) + $9 = $12

**Figure 4–3.** Dangers of Suboptimization

or to use another transfer price method. If the marketing unit is required to buy from the refining unit and is evaluated on its profit performance, the profits will be inflated. The reason is that the marketing unit does not bear the transaction costs of negotiating for and purchasing the products it sells. (The elimination of transaction costs is one of the reasons companies choose to integrate vertically.) In addition, the refining unit receives no credit for the ultimate profits of the corporation.

Finally, because the refining unit is guaranteed an outlet (the marketing unit) for its products and is guaranteed a price (fully absorbed standard cost), it has no incentive to improve either product quality or production efficiencies. If *actual* costs are used, then improved efficiencies result in lower actual costs and consequently a lower transfer price. The refining unit receives only its actual costs as the transfer price and as costs are reduced, so is the transfer price.

If *standard* fully absorbed costs are used, improved efficiencies require that new standards be implemented. The result will be a new, lower transfer price based on the new, lower standard fully absorbed cost. *Cost-plus* systems are equally ineffective in encouraging efficiencies, because the imputed profit, that is, the "plus" portion, is a percentage of the base costs. Lower costs result in a lower imputed profit.

### Marginal Cost

The problems raised by full cost-based methods led economists to look toward a marginal cost transfer price. Marginal cost is the cost to produce one more unit of a product. Transfer pricing systems based on marginal costs rely on economic models (figure 4–4). The earliest and most often quoted economic model related to transfer pricing was developed by Jack Hirschleifer. His model also offers an alternative to a market-based transfer price when the market for the product to be transferred is either imperfectly competitive or does not exist.

The objective of the Hirschleifer model is to determine the optimum joint level of output for the refining and marketing units. He points out that the optimum level can be reached by mandate from centralized management or by

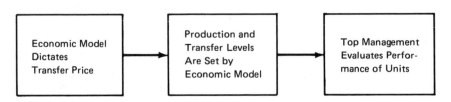

**Figure 4–4.** Marginal Cost Transfer Price

determining the price at which the product should be transferred from the refining to the marketing unit.

Determination of the optimum output and transfer price is shown in figure 4-5. The output volume is measured on the horizontal axis, and the prices and costs for the product are shown on the vertical axis. For simplification, the market is considered to be perfectly competitive as indicated by the horizontal demand curve *MQ*. The curve labeled *mmc* represents the marginal marketing cost, and the curve *mrc* represents the marginal refining cost as a function of the output of each business unit.

Assuming that the market is competitive, the marketing unit will face a ruling price *P*. The optimal solution for the corporation is to produce at the level where the overall marginal costs of refining and marketing (*mrc* + *mmc*) equal the ruling price *P*. If *P* is equal to the distance from the axis to the demand curve (*MO*), then *P* equals *OM*, and the optimum output is *OL*. For the range where *mrc* exceeds the average variable cost, the marginal refining cost is also the price at which the refining unit would be willing to transfer the product to the marketing unit.

The optimal output level (*OL*) can be reached two ways: by mandate or by correct transfer pricing. The output level can be mandated if central management calculates the total marginal costs of the refining and marketing units (*mrc* + *mmc*) and determines the point where they intersect with the demand curve (*MQ*). The intersection establishes *OL* as the optimal output level.

Individual managers will arrive at the same decision if the refining business unit calculates its marginal costs (*mrc*) and uses that schedule as its transfer price (*p\**) at any given quantity of output. Knowing the ruling price *P*, the marketing unit can calculate its marginal revenue (*P-p\**) at various levels of output. The point where the marketing unit's marginal revenue equals its marginal cost (*mmc*) is the optimal quantity that it will buy from the refining unit. As indicated on the graph in figure 4-5, the output level is *OL*, the same as that dictated by central management. The process remains the same if the market for the product is not perfectly competitive. In that case, a sloping demand curve would replace the horizontal line *MQ*, and optimal output would be determined by setting the sum of the marginal costs for refining and marketing equal to the marginal revenue in the final market.

The marginal cost rule for determining appropriate transfer prices is a useful way to approach the problem of optimizing a company's performance. There are, however, several problems that must be addressed. Determining the slope of the demand curve and calculating long-run marginal costs and revenues can be very difficult tasks, particularly in an environment of price controls. If more than one refinery produces a given product, or more than one marketing unit buys it, the marginal cost rule will not work. Marginal costs for each refining and each marketing unit may differ, and, therefore, no one ideal production level can be established for the corporation. Nevertheless, the marginal cost method high-

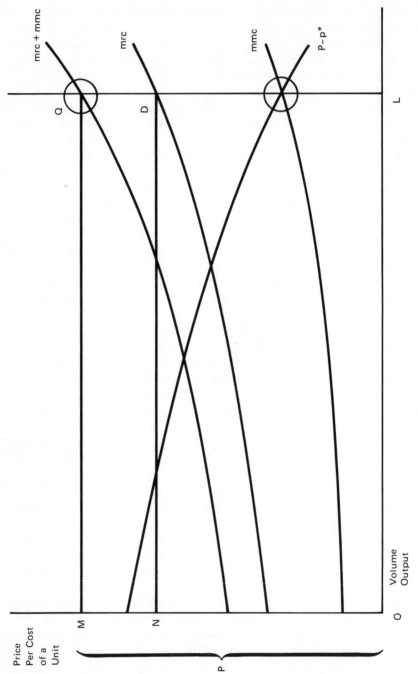

**Figure 4–5.** Marginal Cost–Optimum Output

lights two useful concepts: costs vary with the level of production, and manufacturing and marketing activities are linked closely together in determining the overall performance of a corporation.

### Two-Step Approach

The two-step approach begins to address the issues of decentralized decision making and measuring the profit performance of individual business units. Using this method, the transfer price is made up of two parts: a guaranteed retainer fee paid by the transferee (marketing) to the transferor (refining) designed to cover fixed costs and profits, and a charge for the standard variable cost of each unit (figure 4–6).

The distinguishing characteristic of the two-step approach is the retainer fee. It is negotiated by the two unit managers with the approval of top management. The two-step method is the first one that recognizes that the corporate profit on the sale of the end product should be split between the refining and the marketing business units because each plays a vital role in creating and selling the product. The retainer also contains a provision for profit, giving the refining unit features of a profit center.

There are several reasons the refining unit is not a true profit center, however. First, the refining and marketing managers can arrange a fee that would not be appropriate in a true free market environment. Second, because the fee is fixed for the negotiated time period, the refining unit is guaranteed a set profit regardless of the market price fluctuations that the marketing unit is experiencing. While the two-step approach gives the appearance that refining is a profit center, in fact, it is not. Top management's decisions regarding the refinery are not and should not be made on imputed profits. Therefore, the measure of the refining unit's performance usually goes back to the basics: measuring the unit as a cost center.

### Market Price

The two-step approach begins to provide the types of information necessary to evaluate the profitability of the refining and marketing units as if they were independent companies. It fails, however, because the retainer fee does not represent an outside market.

If the profit centers were independent companies, any transfer of product would require a market place transaction recorded at the current market price. Transferring a product at the market price reflects the cost that the marketing unit would have to bear if the product were not produced within the corporation.

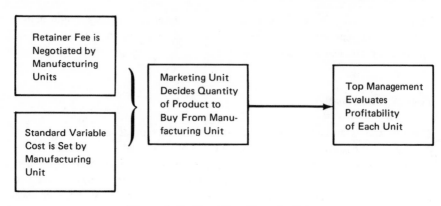

**Figure 4-6.** Two-Step Transfer Price

A market price also reflects the price that the refining unit would receive if it sold the product outside the corporation. If the business units are allowed to buy and sell outside the corporation, each manager can use the third party supplier and customer sales prices as the basis for a decision to trade with the other unit. Top management can judge each business unit on its profit performance based on the results of those decisions (figure 4–7).

Although the market price concept is simple and straightforward, implementation may be a problem because a market price may not be readily discernible. If the refining unit must meet the marketing function's supply needs before it can sell to third parties, it may not have an accurate third party–based market price to use as a transfer price. For example, the refining unit of ABC Oil Company produces 1,000 barrels a day, 500 of which are transferred to the mar-

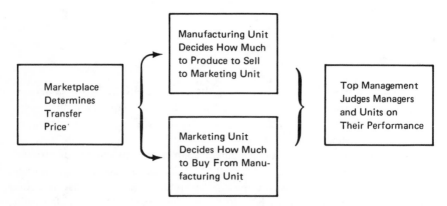

**Figure 4-7.** Market-Based Transfer Price

keting unit. The other 500 barrels are sold in 50 barrel lots to ten independent marketing companies.

The market price that the refining unit receives from the ten independents may not be an accurate transfer price for the 500 barrels that are transferred to the marketing unit because the volumes of each sale are one-tenth as great; the internal transfer requires no marketing efforts by the refining unit; no credit terms are required for the internal transfers. Therefore, the refining and marketing units will negotiate an adjustment to the market price to arrive at a transfer price that satisfies both units.

The refining and marketing units may also refer to published prices as the basis for a market transfer price. The published prices are more useful for assisting with periodic business unit performance evaluation than operating decisions regarding supply source because of the lag time and the unvalidated nature of price series publication. A published price is rarely suitable for use as a transfer price unless adjustments are made. The reason is that published prices are often for products that are slightly different or involve contracts that reflect delivery, quantity, or other nonstandard features. In the oil industry, companies adjust published prices primarily to account for transportation differences and credit terms.

Another problem that occurs when basing transfer prices on market prices is that market prices may fluctuate so often that companies spend a great deal of time adjusting a transfer price to match the market price changes.

David Solomons, in his book entitled *Divisional Performance,* provides an excellent discussion of the difficulty and problems associated with market-based transfer pricing. His analysis uses break-even analysis graphics to highlight these problems. Following is a summary adaptation of that analysis using the ABC Oil Company as the illustrative case. In figure 4-8, ABC's marketing unit uses oil products transferred from ABC's refinery unit, as well as oil products purchased in a competitive market from outside suppliers. In figure 4-9 ABC's refinery unit is producing more oil products than the marketing unit wants and is selling the excess production on the outside market. In both cases, units of product produced or sold are measured horizontally, and dollars of revenue or cost per unit are measured vertically.

On figure 4-8, the horizontal line $P_B$ represents the demand curve for the final product of the marketing unit.

For purposes of this discussion, the market is assumed to be perfectly competitive, implying that the price per barrel obtainable by ABC's marketing unit is independent of the quantity sold, since the marketing unit's sales do not represent more than a small part of the total industry sales of the products. From the unit revenue $P_B$, the marketing unit must recover the distribution and sales costs. These sales costs consist of fixed costs of operating service stations, together with the variable costs per unit of selling products to the retail market. The fixed costs will determine long-term issues, such as whether to build new service sta-

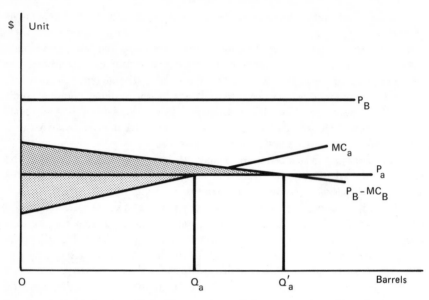

**Figure 4-8.** Marketing Unit Economics of Intracompany Transfers versus Open Market Sales

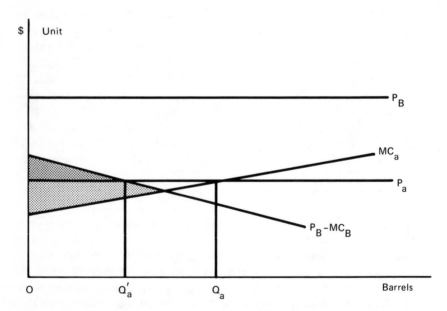

**Figure 4-9.** Refinery Unit Economics of Intracompany Transfers versus Open Market-Sales

tions and whether to continue operating certain existing stations. They do not determine short-term questions such as level of sales once the service station is in place. In pursuing these short-term questions, fixed costs are ignored and incremental costs are analyzed. How these incremental costs react to changes in capacity utilization varies from station to station, market area to market area.

The discussion also assumes that incremental costs increase as capacity utilization increases, because labor requirements and, thus, costs increase to meet the expansion. Figure 4-8 does not show the incremental cost of selling. However, the balance remaining of the sales revenue (per unit) after meeting costs is shown by the line $P_B - MC_B$, which is the price of the refined product minus the marginal cost of selling the product. The line slopes from left to right, because an increasing marginal cost of selling the product is being deducted from a constant selling price per unit of the final product. The line represents the net revenue earned by the marketing unit for each additional unit of the product it sells, subject to the recovery of its fixed costs and to the further deduction of the product costs it uses, whether the product is bought outside or obtained by transfer from the refinery unit of ABC Oil Company.

ABC's refinery costs can be broken out into fixed and variable over the levels of output. Fixed costs play the same role for the refining unit as they do for the marketing unit. They determine whether refinery capacity is brought on stream, but do not determine at what capacity utilization level the refinery will be maintained. Since this is the relevant question, we must focus our attention on the variable costs of the refining unit, which are shown by line $MC_a$. It is shown as rising as refinery utilization expands, since we assume more expensive refining techniques are involved as production increases. The ABC refinery unit is not the only source of the oil products. Unlimited products can also be purchased on the open market at a price of $P_a$ per barrel.

Figure 4-8 shows the correct course of action for the marketing unit and the refinery unit. The marketing unit should sell products so long as, by doing so, the marketing unit makes a profit contribution (incremental costs are less than incremental revenues). A profit contribution is made by the marketing unit up to $OQ'_a$ barrels so long as it pays no more than the market price $P_a$ whether its supplies come from ABC's refining unit or from the outside market. The selling of oil products in excess of $OQ'_a$ results in a negative profit contribution. Selling less than quantity $OQ'_a$ results in foregone profit opportunities.

The refining unit of ABC should supply only $OQ_a$ units at Price $P_a$. Supplying more than $OQ_a$ will result in a negative profit contribution (shown by line $MC_a$). ABC's marketing unit, therefore, will obtain $OQ_a$ barrels of oil products from an internal transfer from ABC's refining unit, and $Q_aQ'_a$ by purchase on the open market. This supply balance results in an optimal solution as discussed earlier.

If the ABC marketing unit were to obtain more that $OQ_a$ products from an internal transfer of the ABC refining unit, the additional cost to the ABC company of refining costs in excess of the quantity $OQ_a$ would be greater than if ABC bought products outside at the price $P_a$. Alternatively, if the marketing unit were to receive less than $OQ_a$ from the refining unit and bought more from the open market, the ABC Company would again be incurring a greater cost for the products than necessary. Market price, then, is the best method for qualifying opportunity costs and, thus serves as an excellent basis for a transfer price. Market price serves the same role for the ABC's refining unit. Figure 4-9 shows the marketing unit's cost of selling the products to be higher than indicated in figure 4-8.

The line $P_B$ - $MC_B$ slopes at a steeper rate. The marketing unit, therefore, would have a smaller profit contribution from the sale of successive barrels of refined product than indicated in figure 4-8.

This situation forces line $P_B$ - $MC_B$ to intersect the line $P_a$ to the left of the point where $MC_a$ intersects it. This, of course, means that at the price $P_a$ which the refinery can wholesale the product for on the outside market, the refinery unit is willing to supply $OQ_a$, the same quantity as in figure 4-8 because refining up to that quantity results in a profit contribution. Up to that refinery utilization level, the line $MC_a$ is below the line $P_a$. The marketing unit is prepared to accept only the quantity $OQ'_a$, for to transfer more would result in a negative profit contribution for the marketing uni. The line $P_B$ - $MC_B$ is below the line $P_a$ at all points to the right of $Q'_a$. Since the ABC refinery can profitably refine $OQ_a$, but the marketing unit can absorb only $OQ'_a$ profitably at the price $P_a$, the refinery unit should sell $Q'_a Q_a$ products to the outside market.

In figures 4-8 and 4-9, the refinery unit's profits, subject to fixed costs, are represented by the vertically hatched area, while the marketing unit's profits, subject to fixed costs, are represented by the area of horizontal hatching. Figures 4-8 and 4-9 point out the advantages of using a market price to achieve optimization of the company's resources. The problems of using an unrealistic price should also be discussed.

For purposes of discussion, we will continue with our example of the ABC refining and marketing units. Figure 4-10 shows the line $MR_B$ - $MC_B$ representing the marginal net revenue obtained by the marketing unit from the sale of successive units of refined products.

$MR_B$ - $MC_B$ reflects that additional value the marketing unit will attach to additional products. The line $MC_a$ shows the marginal cost to the ABC refinery unit of expanding capacity utilization. The horizontal line $P_a$ shows the transfer price that has been fixed for the products as they are moved from the refining unit to the marketing unit. At price $P_a$, the marketing unit will only accept quantity $OQ'_a$, while the refining unit will refine products to quantify $Q'_a Q_a$ and sell it on the open market at price $P_a$. However, suppose that product demand is soft on the open market for the additional products because of the excess costs associated with selling them. The open market would absorb the

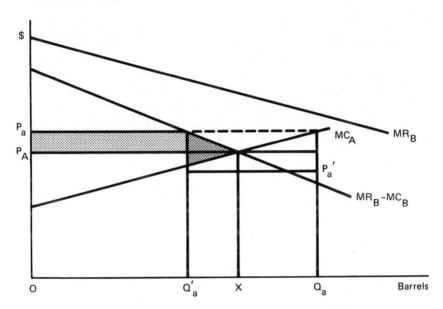

**Figure 4-10.** Problems with Market-based Transfer Prices

excess product at a lower price $P_a'$. At the ruling transfer price $P_a$, the refining unit will limit its output to $OQ_a'$. If, however, the transfer price had been set at $P_A$ instead of $P_a$, the refining unit would have been content to produce an extra volume $Q_a'X$ of product since its marginal costs would still be covered. The marketing unit would still accept the product because it could still make a profit contribution by selling it. The ABC Oil Company would have been better off as a result of the output to the extent of the extra profits represented by the shaded triangle. This is the amount by which the aggregate profits of the units would together have increased.

The change in the transfer price from $P_a$ to $P_A$ would *not* have improved the profits of both units equally. At the lower transfer price of $P_A$, the area of the shaded triangle will be divided between the two divisions, so that the profits below the line $P_A$ will go to the refining unit. Its new total profit, subject to fixed costs, is shown by the triangle bounded by the vertical axis, line $P_A$ and line $MC_A$, while the part above line $P_A$ will go to the marketing unit whose total profit, subject to fixed costs, is now shown by the triangle bounded by the vertical axis, lines $P_A$ and $MR_B - MC_B$. However, while the refining unit gains its share of the shaded triangle when the transfer price is reduced, it loses the whole of the vertically hatched rectangle. Its gain from increased volume is offset by the reduced transfer price it gets from the whole of its output. The marketing unit, on the other hand, gains both from the increase in its volume and from the reduction in the transfer price it has to pay for the products. The marketing unit's gain is greater than refinery unit's loss. The ABC Oil Company is better off as a result of the change in price.

The analysis depicted here highlights the importance of understanding the goal of optimizing corporate resources, the ramifications of a miscalculated transfer price, and the difficulty of distinguishing between issues such as optimizing corporate resources, cross subsidization, and measuring performance based on profitability. For example, should the manager of the refining unit in the figure 4-10 case be penalized for his or her action? A cursory analysis would show profits to be down by transferring products at the lower transfer price of $P_A$. If only ROI were used as a performance indicator, the refining unit's manager would be penalized. However, if overall company optimization were reviewed, the refining manager would be rewarded for transferring products at the lower price, since it results in increased profits for ABC Company, as shown by the hatched triangle.

The effect of the change in transfer pricing on profitability of the two units need not always result in the situation depicted in figure 4-10. The particular cost and revenue functions determine the effect of a given change in the transfer price of the relative position of two business units.

## Negotiation

If the refining and marketing units were two independent companies, they would negotiate the price of the product changing hands. Negotiation occurs within a corporation when management wants to evaluate both units as profit centers, and when a market price is not available (figure 4-11). Because negotiation of each transaction would be very time-consuming, periodic meetings are normally held at which prices for a range of products are determined. Advocates of negotiated transfer prices point out that negotiation comes as close to the concept of independent companies as is possible in an integrated corporation. Negotiation creates a forum for each unit manager to discuss his or her particular operating constraints. It is also flexible, allowing the price to change as the market or internal capacity conditions change.

Although negotiation may be the optimal solution for a corporation that wants unit managers to be the major decision makers, the method has several disadvantages. Negotiation can be time-consuming. Major negotiations may be required for a myriad of products, pulling managers to the bargaining table when their talents could be better used in their operations. Second, because each manager has his or her own priorities, negotiation may be a divisive process that perpetuates rather than resolves internal corporate conflicts. A transfer price

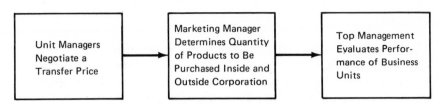

**Figure 4-11.** Negotiated Transfer Price

method should supply information that enables managers to make decisions that are in the best interests of the corporation. Negotiation may not always do that.

*Linear Programming*

Linear programming refers to mathematical models that translate corporate costs and resources and market conditions into linear equations (figure 4-12). By solving the multiple mathematical equations, a manager can arrive at the optimal production level for the company. Each solution is unique, based on the specific set of variables (corporate costs and resources) and includes a dual solution of shadow prices. The shadow prices are the derived transfer prices that, when used, result in the corporation operating at the optimal production level.

Linear programming is a useful tool that allows a corporation to model its activities given different corporate resource and market constraints. The strength of linear programming is that it recognizes that changing resources and market conditions can affect the outcome of a decision. A decision regarding resource allocation is appropriate for a particular set of circumstances, in a set time period, given resource and market conditions that fit the situation. Although linear programming is a valuable tool for corporate analysis, its complexity and situational nature make it inappropriate for public policy analysis.

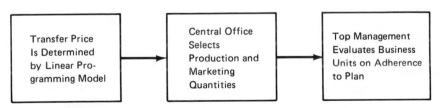

**Figure 4-12.** Linear Programming Generated Transfer Price

**Summary**

Transfer pricing is the only way that revenue can be assigned to products that move from one business unit to another in the same company. The accounting profession does not recognize revenue until a sale is made to an external legal entity. For a variety of internal reasons, it is sometimes desirable to estimate the value of a product before it leaves the corporation and enters the marketplace. The value is only an estimate, however, and does not carry the validity of a marketplace transaction.

Corporations use any and all of the six methods described here for a variety of purposes, including resource allocation and management control. No method is perfect. Each meets the needs of some corporations in some circumstances. As table 4-1 illustrates, four of the six methods discussed here allow for profit performance analysis of both the refining and marketing units. However, two of these methods should be viewed with caution. The two-step approach enables the refining unit to be a pseudo-profit center. In actual practice, performance evaluation usually falls back to a cost-based system. Linear programming offers unique answers to specific decisions that an individual corporation faces. The shadow prices that are generated are not transferrable to other decisions or different corporations. Only market price and strict negotiation come close to imitating the marketplace transaction that would have occurred if both units were independent companies.

Fourteen oil companies were interviewed to determine how transfer pricing systems are used in the oil industry. Details of some of these interviews are discussed in the next chapter. The oil companies that were interviewed had designed transfer pricing systems to meet the purposes discussed earlier in this section.

One major oil company attempts to anticipate problems in major product lines by monitoring gross profit trends. Using a market-based transfer price, the company can estimate gross profits, then focus its investigative resources on areas where the system indicates there may be a problem. Another uses the market price method to point out potential problem areas in its operations. The profit and loss statements generated by that company's system are viewed as diagnostic reports. Trouble spots are then investigated carefully before a decision to change any phase of the operations is made. No change is made based solely on the profit and loss statement derived from a transfer pricing system. A third company transfers all of its products from the refining to the marketing unit at standard full-absorbed cost, with the belief that refining, as a manufacturer of the product, should not receive any credit for products sold by the marketing unit.

A corporation continually evaluates its organizational structure to determine if it matches its corporate strategy. A corporation also continually looks at decisions regarding transfer pricing. If a system is in use, should it be continued? Is the information being generated meaningful? Should a different method be

**Table 4-1**
**Summary of Transfer Price Methods**

| Name of Method | Basis of Transfer Price | Basis of Unit Analysis | | Benefits of Method | Problems with Method |
|---|---|---|---|---|---|
| | | Refining | Marketing | | |
| Cost-based | Refining unit's cost to produce | Cost | Profit | Costs are usually collected already for accounting purposes. Managers can easily understand how they are being evaluated. | Refining unit is a cost center. Method assumes constant levels of costs. |
| Marginal cost | Refining unit's marginal cost to produce product | Cost | Profit | Recognizes that costs vary with the level of production | Difficulty of determining demand curves. Manufacturing unit is a cost center. |
| Two-step approach | Lump sum retainer fee plus variable costs of unit refining | Profit | Profit | Recognizes that corporate profits are a result of efforts by refining and marketing units. Recognizes mix of fixed and variable costs. | Retainer fee can be "fixed" by mutual agreement. Marketing unit takes the brunt of market fluctuations. Evaluation of manufacturing unit usually reverts to cost basis. |
| Market-based | Price of an arm's length transaction | Profit | Profit | Closely models a transaction between two independent companies. | Published market prices may not be available. Available market prices may need adjustment to reflect special product or sale characteristics. |
| Negotiation | Result of negotiation between refining and marketing managers | Profit | Profit | Closely models a transaction between two independent companies. Allows price to change as the market or internal capacity conditions change. Encourages interaction between refining and marketing managers. | Negotiation may be time consuming and divisive. |
| Linear programming | Shadow price solution of individual linear programming model | Profit | Profit | Recognizes that decisions requiring optimal corporate performance rely on a multitude of factors. | Transfer prices are a function of different corporate resources and market constraints, and vary from company to company. |

employed? Should transfer pricing be discontinued? A corporation that does not use transfer pricing will also reassess that decision from time to time. The final decision will be based on the corporation's overall business strategy and the operational approach it has taken to implement that strategy.

Monsanto Company recently changed its transfer pricing method and believed that the operational impact was sufficiently important to report to the stockholders. In Monsanto's 1976 Annual Report, the company noted that:

> Following the formation of Monsanto Chemicals Intermediates Company, it was determined that Monsanto Company should change its transfer pricing policy on certain large-volume chemicals such as styrene monomer used in plastics and acrylonitrile used in man-made fibers. Operating units will be charged for these products at cost rather than at market price. As a result shareholders will have a better perception and understanding of the integrated nature of Monsanto's business. This decision has no effect on corporate operating results, but it does affect the operating results of six Monsanto operating units. Accordingly, line profit results for the past five years have been restated to reflect the change.

Corporations recognize the impact that an inappropriate transfer price can have on internal decision making and, consequently, on meeting corporate objectives. Managers are sensitive to the potential problem of transfer pricing, which is a fragile link between business units. Business decisions based on transfer pricing are approached with extreme caution. Major oil companies that have spent twenty years developing sophisticated transfer pricing systems still use them for diagnostic rather than decision-making purposes.

Extrapolating a corporate transfer pricing system to an entire industry for broad-based policy purposes should also be approached with caution. Specialized systems designed to meet one corporation's requirements may be totally unsuited to another corporation's structure and strategy. In the next chapter, we examine current transfer pricing practices in the oil industry.

**Notes**

1. Gordon Shillinglaw, *Managerial Cost Accounting,* fourth edition, (Homewood, Ill., Irwin Press, 1977.)

# 5

## Current Transfer Pricing Practices in the Oil Industry

Transfer pricing systems are often part of a company's effort to gather internal quantitative information for making decisions regarding how to use the company's resources most efficiently. Oil companies are particularly sensitive to accurate data collection because they have large capital investments that must be used efficiently and narrow per unit margins in which to operate.

Oil companies design transfer pricing systems for the purpose of developing internal data necessary for decision making. Like all data collection mechanisms, transfer pricing systems should be viewed with a number of considerations in mind. First, they represent only one source of data. No company makes major operating decisions on the basis of one set of data. Each company continuously compares the results generated by a transfer pricing system with results based on other analytical tools. Second, the systems are normally designed for internal operating purposes. They assist with making decisions on internal activities ranging from diagnosing potential product line profitability problems to capital investments in segments of the company. Finally, each company's system is tailored to meet the specific objectives for which it was designed. Using a transfer pricing system for a purpose other than the one for which it was designed may lead to unwarranted conclusions based on inappropriate data.

These qualifications should be considered when reviewing transfer pricing systems that exist in the oil industry. Many companies in the oil industry have been developing and using transfer pricing systems on a large scale for a long period of time. The purpose of this chapter is to review these systems to determine if they meet or can be adapted to meet the requirements of DOE and other public policy makers.

The authors, in conjunction with DOE staff members, met with eleven integrated oil companies. These eleven companies deal internally with the issue of how their refining and marketing units should be organized and evaluated to ensure that they are contributing optimally to the overall goals and objectives of the corporation. The meetings were intended to establish a dialogue between organizations that have developed expertise in the areas of performance measurements and transfer pricing and the DOE. Specifically, the three major objectives of these meetings were:

To determine how widely transfer pricing systems are used in the oil industry

To examine the purposes for which the systems were designed

To learn the transfer pricing methods on which the systems are based

The discussions focused on the organization, operations, and interactions of the petroleum refining and marketing units of the company. Other segments of the petroleum business, such as exploration and production, were set aside. All nonpetroleum and foreign operations were likewise not part of the discussions. Systems that computed taxes for foreign subsidiaries or other external reports were not reviewed in detail, because these systems do not correspond to the purposes of public policy makers.

Each meeting began with a general discussion of the company's corporate strategy and structure as they related to the two business units. Particular attention was given to changes in corporate strategy and the corresponding changes in corporate structure and performance measurement systems.

If the company used a transfer pricing system, documentation of the methodology, problems, and successes that the company has faced with the system was requested. If the company did not use transfer pricing, documentation regarding the decision not to use it was requested. Summaries of the discussions with the seven oil companies that had transfer pricing systems are included in this chapter. To preserve the confidentiality of internal information systems, we refer to the interviewees as Companies A through G.

The authors also interviewed three independent gasoline marketers. Independent oil companies without refineries do not have the problem of optimizing the interaction between the refining and marketing units. Therefore, they do not need nor do they use a transfer pricing system.

Independent marketers rely on refineries of both independent and integrated companies for the source of their petroleum products. Their purchases represent the major external market for petroleum products. A transfer pricing system that is market-based requires access to either published prices or marketplace transactions. The transactions between major integrated oil companies and independent marketers represent the major source of actual marketplace transactions for a market-based transfer price.

Independent marketers were helpful in defining the structure and the operation of the wholesale gasoline distribution system. In particular, discussions with independent oil companies centered around the way the wholesale market functions, including relevant geographical markets and the numbers of transactions that occur.

## Petroleum Manufacturing and Distribution:
## A Systems Description

Understanding the physical structure of the refining (manufacturing) and marketing (wholesale and retail distribution) sectors is a key to the analysis of the integrated oil company interviews. To this end, a brief overview of the dimensions of these sectors follows.

Refineries, representing the primary users of crude oil, are designed to turn crude oil into a wide variety of commercial products. These products include gasoline, propane, butane, and feedstocks such as benzene, xylene, and propylene. Such products are said to come from the "top of the crude" barrel. Other products include the middle distillates—home heating oil, diesel fuel, jet fuel, and kerosene—and the heavy products—residual fuel oil, petroleum coke, and asphalt. Gasoline accounts for 40 to 50 percent of domestic refinery capacity utilization.

The marketing sector of the petroleum industry represents the network of wholesalers (jobbers), fuel oil dealers, and retail service station operators who distribute the products to the consumer. This discussion focuses on gasoline because it is the dominant product in the market.[a]

The refined petroleum product known as motor gasoline enters the marketplace from three major sources: major vertically integrated refiners, who have operations in exploration, production, refining, transportation, and marketing; independent refiners, who concentrate their activities in refining and may also have marketing activities; and foreign refiners who import to the United States. Foreign refinery imports represent less than 3 percent of the market and are not reviewed here.

As gasoline flows out of the refinery, it is either stored in product terminals next to the refinery or transported by tankers, barges, trucks, or pipelines to storage points to await distribution decisions. An insignificant amount of gasoline is sold directly to the end user prior to this point. (Some refineries, for example, locate service stations next to the refinery for direct end-use sales.)

When gasoline is shipped via common carrier pipelines, the gasoline is commingled with other gasoline and loses its brand-name identity. The shipper simply withdraws gasoline of certain specifications at the destination point.

The manager who makes the decision to store gasoline at the refinery product terminals, to sell it directly to a customer, or to transport it to a distribution point for sale to a variety of customers, must consider what would be the optimal decision for the business unit and the entire company. The alternatives are displayed in figure 5-1.

Two-thirds of all gasoline refined in the United States is delivered in dealer tank wagons through refinery-owned terminals and bulk plants.[1]

Individual companies vary in the percent of gasoline output distributed in this manner. These distribution channels are represented by patterns A, B, C,

---

[a]Information in this section is based on our interviews and two source documents: *Final Report, Findings and Views Concerning the Mandatory Petroleum Allocation and Price Regulations,* Federal Energy Administration, Office of Regulatory Programs, September, 1977; and *Gasoline Marketing: Structure, Facts, Demographics,* American Petroleum Institute, December, 1976.

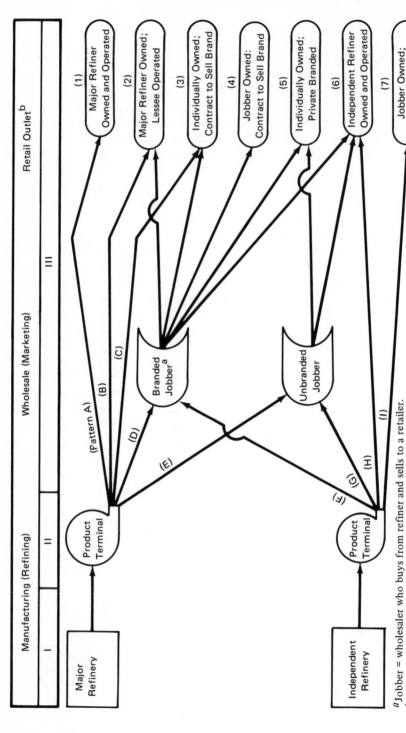

$^a$Jobber = wholesaler who buys from refiner and sells to a retailer.
$^b$Outlet = service station or pump where gasoline is sold to end consumer.

**Figure 5-1.** Gasoline Distribution System.

H, and I on figure 5-1. Intermediate whoesalers (jobbers) account for the balance of gasoline distribution (patterns D, E, F, and G). These wholesalers purchase products at a discount, transport them to bulk storage facilities, and deliver them to retail service stations.

Figure 5-1 shows two types of jobbers: the branded jobbers and the unbranded jobbers. The branded jobbers have the largest share of the jobber market. They buy and resell gasoline under a company brand name. The unbranded jobbers purchase any brand and sell to any branded or unbranded retail outlet. Integrated oil companies or independent refiners that own few and widely scattered service stations (retail outlets) will probably choose to distribute their products through jobbers.[2]

Retail gasoline outlets can be categorized into three main groups: stations affiliated with major oil companies selling major brand gasoline, (figure 5-1, Retail Outlets 1 through 4); stations affiliated with independent refiners (figure 5-1, Retail Outlet 7), and stations operated by nonintegrated independent marketing companies (figure 5-1, Retail Outlets 5 and 6).

Major oil companies own and operate many service stations, using salaried managers (Retail Outlet 1). In the majority of cases, however, the major companies lease the service station to independent business people (Retail Outlet 2). The major oil companies also have franchise agreements with dealers who own their own stations (Retail Outlet 3).

The number of retail outlets has declined in recent years, as integrated oil companies have shifted to fewer service stations that have high volumes. The greatest impact has been the change in the number of lessee and contract retail outlets (figure 5-1, Retail Outlets 2 and 3). In 1972, the FEA Refiner Survey reported 41,159 open or lessee gasoline dealers in the United States. By December 1976, the number had dropped to 9,377.[3] During the same time period, the number of retail outlets owned and operated by major integrated oil companies decreased to a lesser degree, from 3,328 to 1,423.[4] These statistics were confirmed in annual reports of and interviews with integrated oil companies. Several companies discussed efforts to change the patterns of gasoline distribution, reducing the total number of retail outlets under their control and concentrating efforts on owned and operated stations. Nonbranded (independent) marketers (Retail Outlets 4 through 7) usually own and operate their retail outlets with salaried managers, in the same manner that integrated oil companies operate in Distribution Pattern A.

Throughout the oil company interviews, the authors noted the differences among companies in how each distribution system was designed and implemented. Two major points of difference were the responsibilities of the business unit called marketing and the point at which the refining unit ends and the marketing unit begins in the distribution system (Areas I, II, and III in figure 5-1).

Many integrated oil companies considered marketing to be the distribution of gasoline directly to retail outlets. This concept is represented by patterns A, B, and C in figure 5-1. Refining business units in these companies are usually responsible for distribution patterns D and E.

Some companies consider product terminals as factory warehouses. These companies would include the activities of the refineries and the product terminal (Areas I and II in figure 5-1) in the activities of the refining unit. The marketing unit would include all activities in Area III in the figure.

Alternatively, companies may consider product terminals to be an integral part of the distribution system and include them in the marketing business unit. In these companies, the refining unit's activities would be restricted to Area I, and the marketing unit's responsibilities would begin earlier and include Areas II and III.

## Methods Used and Purposes They Meet

The discussions with oil companies brought divergent viewpoints regarding strategy, structure, and the use of transfer pricing systems. Several companies used transfer pricing systems in the past, but had discarded them when a new corporate structure was implemented. Others had periodically considered implementing a transfer pricing system, but had determined that other management tools were more appropriate for internal planning and operating purposes.

Of the eleven integrated companies that the authors interviewed, seven companies currently use transfer pricing systems. The methods employed varied with the purpose of the system (table 5-1). This is consistent with the concept that a corporation's structure is designed to support its strategy, and that performance measurement systems must be designed to support the purposes for which they are developed.

Each company that the authors interviewed had a different corporate strategy and a particular structural framework through which the company operated. Based on the company's structure, top management had evaluated the applicability of a transfer pricing system to operate the company efficiently. Those companies that chose not to have a transfer pricing system for capital budgeting, product line evaluation, or management control had as many valid reasons as those who decided that a transfer pricing system would be useful to them.

Although the survey did not include all companies in the oil industry, the results provide several important insights into the industry's use of transfer pricing.

All companies (integrated and independent) agree that the complexity of the petroleum product market prevents information based on transfer

**Table 5-1**
**Use of Transfer Pricing in the Oil Industry**

| Company | Purpose of Transfer Pricing System | Transfer Pricing Method On Which System Is Based |
|---|---|---|
| A | Assist with capital budgeting. | Market price. Price of gasoline to unbranded resellers. |
| B | Evaluate product lines in order to highlight problem areas for detailed analysis. | Varies by product, but mainly market price. |
| C | Evaluate performance of business units. | Standard full cost. |
| D | Optimize refining and marketing as one combined business unit. | Linear programming. |
| E | Evaluate performance of business units. | Market price. Price of third party sales from major outlet plus negotiated adjustments. |
| F | Evaluate performance of business units. | Market price. Price of third party sales. |
| G | Highlight problem areas for detailed analysis. | Market price. Published prices plus negotiated adjustments. |

pricing systems from being the sole basis for decision making. The system must be supplemented with other performance measures.

A company's decision regarding the potential use of transfer pricing is based on its organizational structure and its information requirements.

Given the system's purpose, a particular transfer pricing method is chosen as the basis for developing the actual transfer pricing formula.

Once a transfer pricing method is selected, a system for using that method to calculate a transfer price is developed.

No individual oil company's transfer pricing system can be transplanted to the federal government for application to all oil companies. Each system is company specific and does not lend itself to alteration. Each system that we reviewed had been designed to provide accounting information that a company believed to be necessary to operate most efficiently. As information requirements change, so do the transfer pricing systems that support them.

*Company A*

Company A is a large vertically and horizontally integrated company that operates in thirty-four countries. Approximately 60 percent of Company A's total income in 1976 was petroleum related, consisting mainly of domestic petroleum operations.

Company A is organized such that its refining and marketing activities are separate functions within the division (figure 5-2).[b] That division is part of the petroleum group. The downstream activities division is a profit center, but the individual functions that make up the division are cost centers. Figure 5-3 depicts the operational flows of Company A's refining and marketing functions.

Company A's United States refining function, which includes product terminals, is responsible for: refining the appropriate volumes of products to meet the needs of Company A's marketing function; and marketing other petroleum products (waxes and asphalt), excluding Company A branded gasoline and home heating oil.

The marketing function's primary activities are the selling of retail-branded gasoline and home heating oil. The home heating oil sales are comparatively small. Its activities begin on the outlet side of the product terminal. When top management evaluates refining and marketing, it combines the revenues that the refining unit receives from its sales to resellers with revenues received by the marketing unit from its retail sales of gasoline and home heating oil. Costs for the two functions as well as those of supply and transportation are likewise combined, so that the profit performance of the downstream activities can be evaluated.

Company A uses a transfer pricing system to assist with capital budgeting decisions. The system was developed to estimate revenues that would result from a proposed capital investment related to gasoline marketing. Gasoline is the main product transferred from the refining function to the marketing function. It is the only product for which a transfer price is estimated. A market-based transfer pricing method is used to calculate the gasoline transfer price. The basis for the market price is the price at which the refining function sells gasoline to unbranded wholesalers.

After analysts have determined the per unit price of gasoline, they subtract the cost of transportation to get the price at which the product would have sold if the sale had been made at the refinery gate. The analysts then add to the price the transportation costs to the major terminal serving the market area in which the transfer is being made. To this price, the analysts add any brand franchise charges. A simplified formula is shown in figure 5-4.

## Company B

Company B is also a multinational corporation, with activities in nearly one hundred countries. It focuses its resources on three major areas: energy, chem-

---

[b]Figures 5-2 through 5-20 are for illustrative purposes and are not exact replicas of corporate organization charts and product distribution systems.

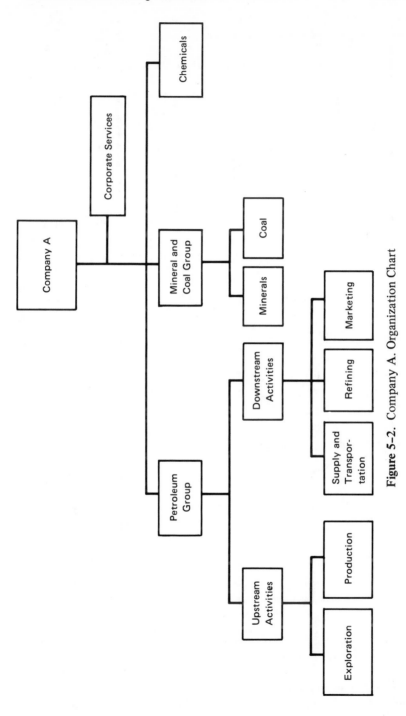

**Figure 5-2.** Company A. Organization Chart

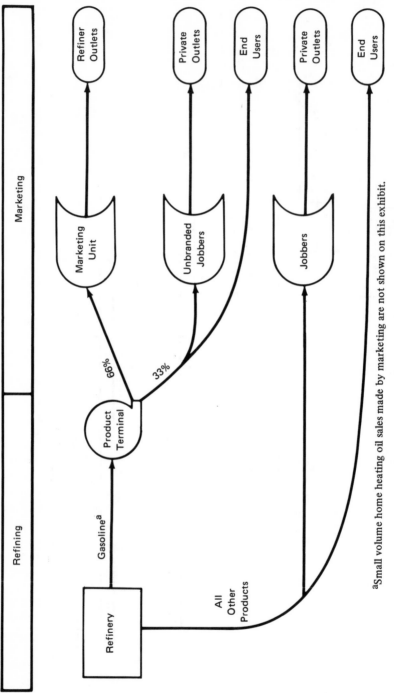

**Figure 5-3.** Company A. Product Distribution System

ªSmall volume home heating oil sales made by marketing are not shown on this exhibit.

Transfer Price = (Unbranded price to third part in same market)  −
(Transportation costs from refinery gate)  +
(Transportation costs to major terminal serving market)  +
(Brand franchise charges)

**Figure 5-4.** Company A. Gasoline Transfer Price Formula

icals, and minerals. As the organizational chart in figure 5-5 illustrates, Company B, like Company A, is both horizontally and vertically integrated. In the 1976 fiscal year, 90 percent of the company's earnings came from petroleum and natural gas operations. The petroleum and natural gas earnings were divided evenly between domestic and foreign operations.

Company B is organized into four groups of activities. Each group contains large business units that are further divided into geographical regions. The basic corporate organization chart appears in figure 5-5. The refining and marketing business units are functions that, when combined, form a larger business unit that is evaluated as a profit center. This organizational structure is similar to that of Company A. There are, however, several differences. The refining and marketing units have different roles and the transfer pricing system that Company B uses serves a different purpose.

Product mixes, that is, quantities of each product to be refined and marketed, are determined by the refining/marketing division. The refining function is responsible for refining products at designated output levels in the most efficient manner. The refining unit sells products directly, but the volumes are not significant. The refining unit's responsibility for products ends at the refinery gate. The division headquarters determines both the most efficient terminal in which to store products and the best mode of transportation to the terminal. After the products arrive at the terminal, they become the responsibility of the marketing unit. The marketing function is responsible for conforming marketing actions to marketing plans in terms of costs and sales volumes. The marketing unit is also expected to determine the best form of transportation for moving products from the terminal to customers. The interaction of the two functions in Company B is illustrated in figure 5-6.

The transfer pricing system that Company B uses was designed as a directional tool. By estimating the value of a product as it leaves the refinery, Company B attempts to track general profit trends of certain product lines for comparative purposes. Reports are compiled on an annual basis. If unfavorable trends are noted, an analyst is assigned to investigate the activity in further detail, using a variety of analytical tools. Nineteen broad product lines have been selected for monitoring. Only products that are *not* subject to federal price con-

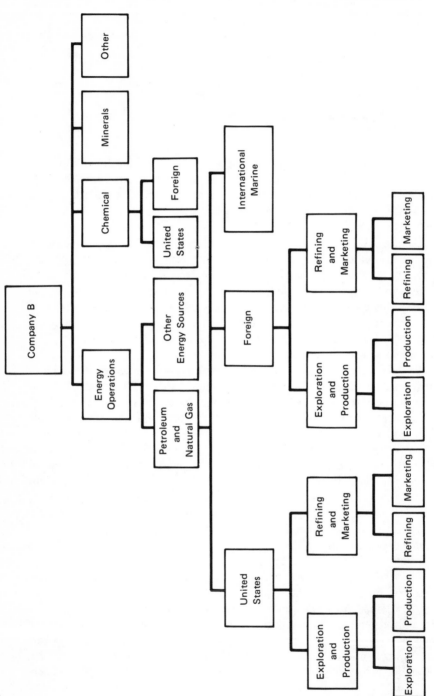

**Figure 5-5.** Company B. Organization Chart

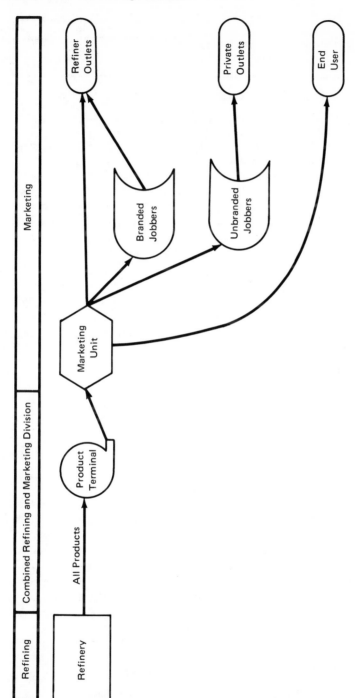

**Figure 5-6.** Company B. Product Distribution System

Transfer Price = (New York cargo price − [(X%) (New York cargo price)]
     − (freight costs)

**Figure 5-7.** Company B. Heating Oil Transfer Price

trols are part of the transfer pricing diagnostic system. Gasoline, therefore, is not currently included in the system.

Company B believes that no one transfer pricing method can be used to calculate the transfer price for all nineteen major products. Most of the calculations attempt to mirror a market price. These market prices are estimated by adjusting either a published price or an actual company transaction to arrive at a refinery gate transfer price. The cost of transporting the product from the refinery gate to the product terminal is charged to marketing in addition to the transfer price. To determine the transfer price for a unit of heating oil, for example, the company uses its New York cargo price minus brokerage fees and freight costs that it did not incur because the product is being transferred internally rather than sold to a third party. Each of the nineteen product groupings has a different formula based on the relevant markets for that group. A simplfied equation is shown in figure 5-7.

*Company C*

Company C is a multinational, fully integrated petroleum company. Its abbreviated organization chart is shown in figure 5-8. Only those activities directly related to petroleum are shown in detail. Although Company C participates in activities outside the petroleum field, petroleum remains the major source of income, representing more than 80 percent of the company's total income in the most recent fiscal year. The income derived from petroleum activities was evenly divided between United States and foreign operations.

The refining and marketing units form a subsidiary that has United States, Asian, and foreign operations. The discussion here centers on the refining and marketing activities in the United States (figure 5-8). The United States operations are organized on a matrix basis, grouped by function and region. Within each region, Company C considers its refining unit to be a function whose sole purpose is to refine products that can be sold by the marketing unit. As soon as the refining process is completed, all products are transferred to the marketing unit. The product terminals, in which products are stored prior to distribution, are the responsibility of the marketing unit (figure 5-9).

A coordinating unit (figure 5-8) ensures that the refining, transportation, and marketing activities are interacting in the manner that is most efficient for

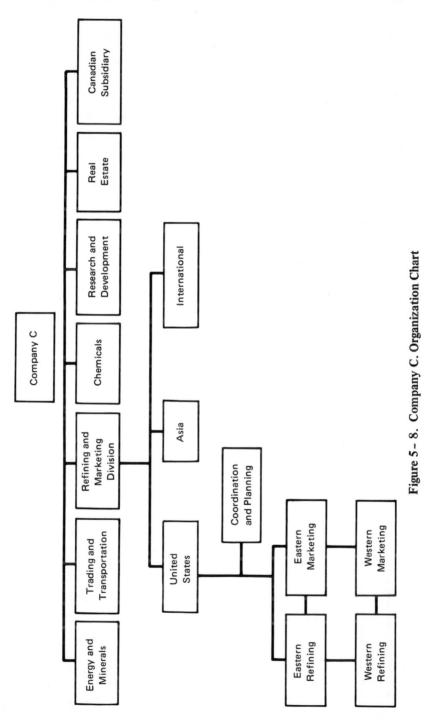

**Figure 5- 8. Company C. Organization Chart**

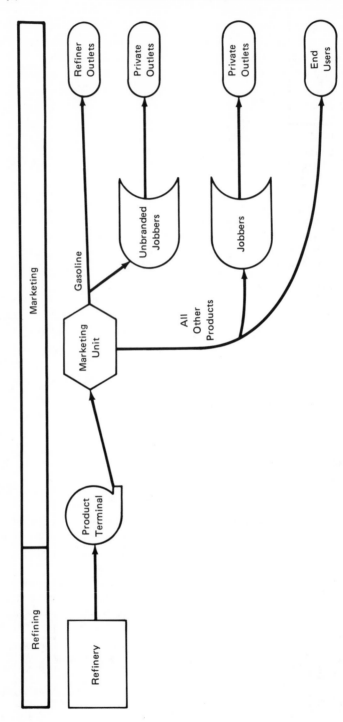

**Figure 5-9.** Company C. Product Distribution System

the regional operations and for the subsidiary. Using this organizational structure, the refining unit is viewed as a cost center. The performance of the unit is evaluated on the basis of its ability to meet planned cost targets.

The marketing unit, considered a profit center, is evaluated in terms of its contribution to profits of the entire company. The unit's revenue figures are readily available from actual third party transactions. Determination of the product costs, however, requires the use of a transfer pricing system. Because the refining unit is considered a cost center, the transfer price system is based on the cost method. Products are transferred from the refining unit to the marketing unit at a price equal to the refining unit's standard costs. Determining the standard costs for petroleum products requires allocation of joint costs. The cost of the raw material, which is crude oil, must be allocated among the products produced during the refinery process. As the schematic diagram of refinery flows in figure 5-10 illustrates, a wide range of products is created during the refining process. Overhead costs and other expenses common to all products must be shared by the products when determining standard product costs. Company C calculates its standard product cost on a quarterly basis, allocating joint costs such as those mentioned here to the primary products.

During periodic reviews of Company C's strategy and corresponding structure, top management has questioned the role of refining and whether it should be given profit responsibility. Each time the decision has been to maintain the current functional organizational framework and to evaluate refining as a cost center and marketing as a profit center. The decision is based on the belief that the current structure and performance evaluation system fit the strategy the company has chosen to pursue.

## Company D

With the exception of some foreign exploration and production activity, Company D focuses its efforts on the United States domestic market. For the most recent fiscal period, upstream operations (oil and gas exploration and production) contributed nearly 60 percent of the company's net income. Oil products represented another 28 percent, with the remainder coming from chemical products and other sources.

The graphic representation of Company D's corporate structure (figure 5-11) is based on conversations with company personnel and a recent annual report. The oil products division, which includes refining, marketing, and transportation, is operated from a matrix configuration. The company coordinates geographical regions as well as product lines and functions. Two-thirds of total refinery output is sold by company-branded service stations. The remainder is sold on the wholesale market.

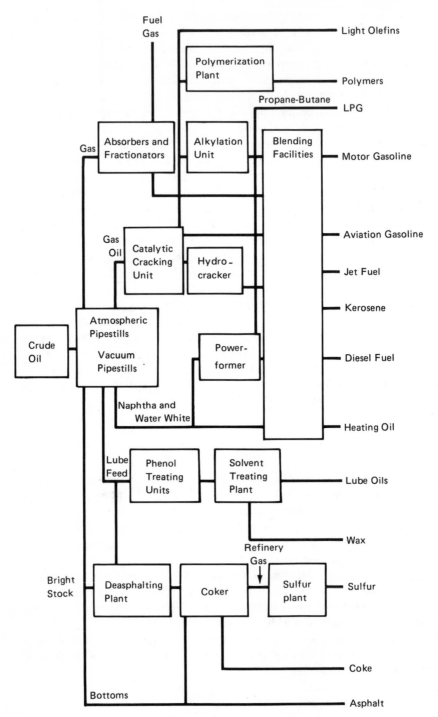

**Figure 5-10.** Refinery Flow Diagram

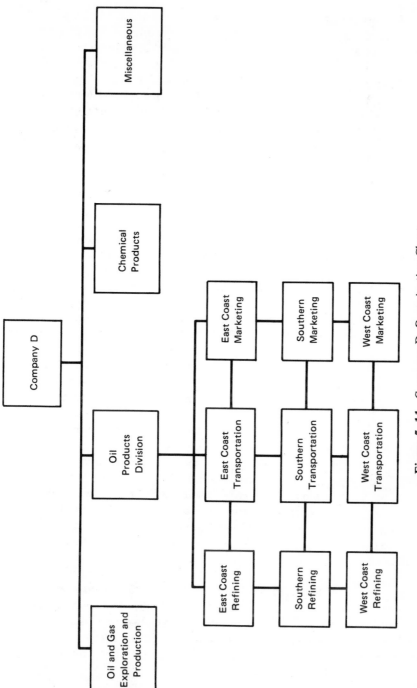

**Figure 5-11.** Company D. Organization Chart

A linear programming model is used to coordinate the activities of three geographical regions that make up the oil products division. The program takes into consideration all of the geographical and resource constraints of Company D, then recommends production levels and distribution patterns that maximize the efficiency of the oil products division. As noted in chapter 4, linear programming is considered to be a type of transfer pricing method because a linear program generates a transfer price for a product at the optimal production level. Using this system, the three functions are cost centers, whose combined activities, making up the oil products division, are evaluated as one profit center.

*Company E*

All of the final three surveyed companies that use transfer pricing systems base them on a market price. However, the source of the market price, the adjustments made to it, and the way that it is used vary by company.

Petroleum operations are the major activity of Company E, providing more than 90 percent of income contribution in the most recent fiscal year. Most of the company's operations are located in the United States, except for minor activity in Canada and several extractive operations overseas. Although Company E will continue to have petroleum as its main line of business, the company is also expanding outside the petroleum field. Its corporate structure, with three large operating groups, reflects that corporate philosophy (figure 5-12). Only the groups that contain United States petroleum activities are shown in detail.

Company E views each of the business units in the three groups as a separate division allowed to make buy and sell decisions. The units are measured in terms of profit performance. Figure 5-13 illustrates the responsibilities of the two divisions concerned with refining and marketing activities.

The petroleum products division is responsible for operating refineries and for marketing petroleum products to industrial and commercial customers and to the wholesale market. The division's major customer in the wholesale market is the marketing division, which currently receives 80-90 percent of the petroleum products division's output of gasoline and home heating oil.

The marketing division is responsible for marketing gasoline and home heating oil to the retail market. The retail market is defined by the company as branded service stations and distributors of the company's branded gasoline and home heating oil. In theory, the marketing division can negotiate with outside suppliers for its products. In practice, however, outside suppliers cannot commit to the large volumes that Company E's marketing division needs because of commitments the suppliers must meet under the federal allocation regulations. Therefore, the marketing division is currently relying on the petroleum products division as its chief supplier.

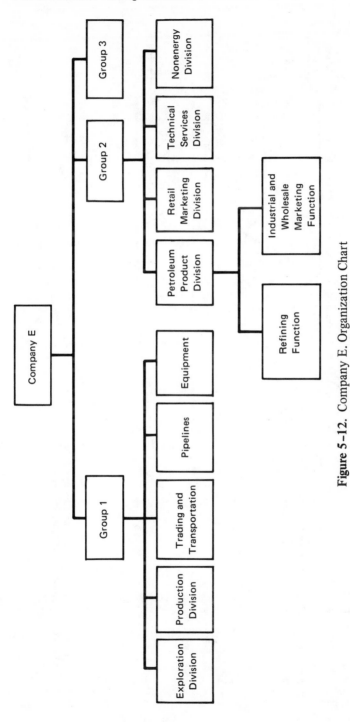

**Figure 5–12.** Company E. Organization Chart

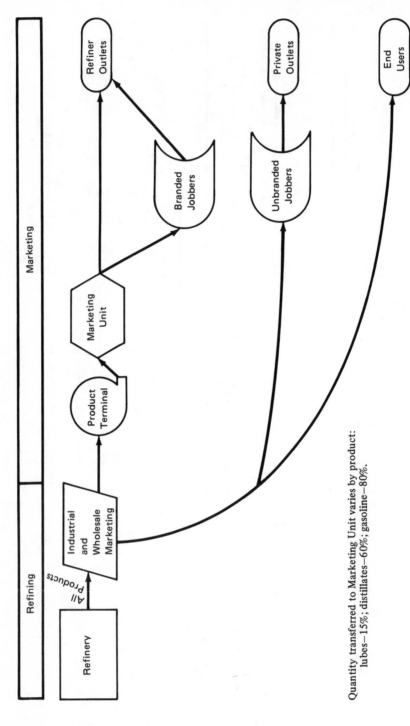

**Figure 5-13.** Company E. Product Distribution System

Quantity transferred to Marketing Unit varies by product:
lubes—15%; distillates—60%; gasoline—80%.

The marketing division also contains activities that are not related to petroleum. These activities are permitted under the decentalized, divisionalized structure that makes up Company E's operating system.

The petroleum products division has a large wholesale market customer base in one major geographical area of the United States. The price at which petroleum products are sold to the wholesale market in that area serves as the basis for the transfer price from the petroleum products division to the marketing division. The actual third party sales price is adjusted, through negotiation, for volume and transportation differences.

The adjustment process varies by product. For gasoline, the base market price is the unit price at which the refining division is selling the product from its largest refinery. To that price is added the cost of transporting the product to the refinery from which the marketing division is making the purchase. Any additional adjustments are made at that point (figure 5–14).

Company E uses the transfer pricing system for the purpose of business unit profit performance evaluation. The system uses the market price method as the basis for calculating the transfer price for gasoline and home heating oil as they move from the petroleum products division to the marketing division.

The marketing division in Company E is currently at a disadvantage in the negotiation process. Although theoretically it can buy from sources other than the petroleum products division, federal allocation regulations make it very difficult to find a supplier who can provide the large quantities it requires to maintain its current level of operations. As an independent company the marketing division could reduce its dependence on a single supplier (refiner) by integrating backward into refining. As a division within Company E, however, the marketing division is not allowed to do that and is, therefore, in a vulnerable negotiating position.

*Company F*

Compnay F concentrates its business activities in the United States, although exploration and production take place throughout the world. The company currently operates within a structure of six major divisions (figure 5–15). For the

---

Transfer Price = (Third party market price at gate of main refinery) + (Transportation costs to refinery from which marketing division is making purchase) ± (Any other credit or volume adjustments)

**Figure 5–14.** Company E. Gasoline Transfer Price

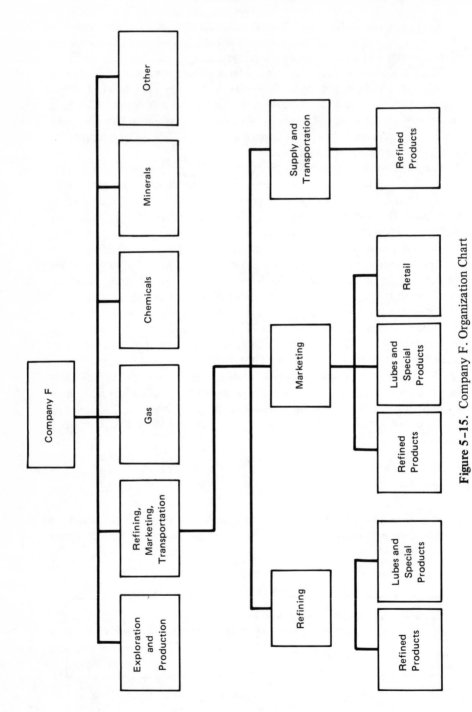

**Figure 5-15.** Company F. Organization Chart

past four years, between 55 and 65 percent of the company's sales have been in the refining, marketing, and transportation division, although the division contributed no more than 11 percent to the company's profits.

The strategy and structure of Company F have been reevaluated and changed over the years. For several years prior to 1975, the refining, marketing, and transportation business units were evaluated as three separate profit centers. A transfer pricing system was used as part of the performance evaluation of the three units. The following discussion of the changes that have occurred in the system focuses on the refining and marketing units.

The first system, which was based on a market price method, relied on Platt's data. A discount factor was applied to Platt's data to arrive at the transfer price. Both the refining and the marketing units were considered profit centers, and the transfer pricing system was part of the performance evaluation system. The refining unit complained about the system because the unit was being penalized for normal seasonal operations. The refineries produced large quantities of gasoline during the late winter in preparation for the spring and summer peak demands. The gasoline price published in Platt's was at its low point during the winter, reflecting low demands. The same problem occurred for fuel oil, which is produced in large quantities in the summer for fall and winter peak demands. As a result, the refining unit's profit figures were low, whereas the marketing unit's profits were inflated. After several refinements to the market-based transfer pricing system, Company F changed its structure so that the refining unit was a cost center and the marketing unit was a profit center. Products were transferred from the refining unit to the marketing unit at break-even cost.

Company F continued to review how it evaluated its business units and determined that a cost-plus method for the transfer pricing system would be appropriate. In a cost-plus method, the refining business unit is reimbursed for its cost and, in addition, receives a specified ROI. The refining unit, therefore, began to take on characteristics of a profit center, and the marketing unit continued as a profit center. The transfer pricing system was later abolished completely. Both the refining and the marketing units were evaluated as cost centers, and no transfer pricing system was required.

Currently, Company F has reduced the number of gasoline refineries it operates and is a net purchaser of gasoline, the only product that requires a transfer pricing system. Lubes and special products are handled by a separate division. The organization chart in figure 5-15 represents the way in which Company F is now organized. Figure 5-16 highlights the activities of the refining and marketing units. The refining unit is responsible for petroleum products until they reach a product terminal. At that point, the products are either sold to a jobber on the wholesale market or are transferred to the marketing unit. The only product that is transferred to the marketing unit is gasoline; 80 percent of the gasoline is sold outside the company, either to jobbers or directly to end users.

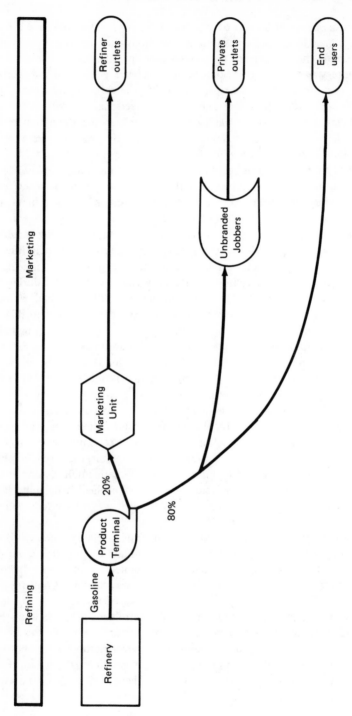

**Figure 5-16.** Company F. Product Distribution System

> Transfer Price = Price at which external sales are made to a similar market.

**Figure 5-17.** Company F. Gasoline Transfer Price Formula

The marketing unit has its own transportation facilities and is responsible for conveying the gasoline to branded retail outlets.

Both the refining and the marketing business units are evaluated as profit centers today. The transfer pricing system that allows both units to be credited with revenues is based on a market price method. The market price used is the same price at which external sales, which account for 80 percent of the refinery unit's output, are made (figure 5-17).

*Company G*

Company G is one of fifteen United States subsidiaries of a major oil company. The parent company has operations throughout the world in all phases of oil exploration, production, refining, and petroleum product marketing. Seventy-eight percent of the parent company's net income in the past fiscal year came from petroleum operations in the United States. As one of the fifteen U.S. subsidiaries, Company G is responsible for domestic refining, transportation, and marketing of petroleum products (figure 5-18). Within Company G, the refining and marketing business units are functions whose activities are controlled by a central planning department. As functions, each business unit has a set of responsibilities and is measured by its adherence to a plan to carry out those responsibilities.

The refining function is strictly the manufacturing arm of Company G. Any marketing activities undertaken by the refining function are for balancing purposes only, when the marketing function cannot handle all of the refining functions' output. The refining unit is responsible for all products until they enter the product terminals (figure 5-19). As noted in the figure, the product terminals are the responsibility of the marketing function. The marketing function handles all sales, including industrial and commercial sales, and sales to branded jobbers and independent jobbers. For gasoline, sales are evenly divided between branded and independent jobbers.

Company G uses a transfer pricing system for diagnostic purposes. If the system points out a potential profitability problem for a product line, three major areas are critically examined by internal analysts: channels of distribution, customer base, and geographical locations of sales. At least four other performance indicators are examined in addition to profits arrived at through the transfer pricing system before the internal analyst begins an investigation.

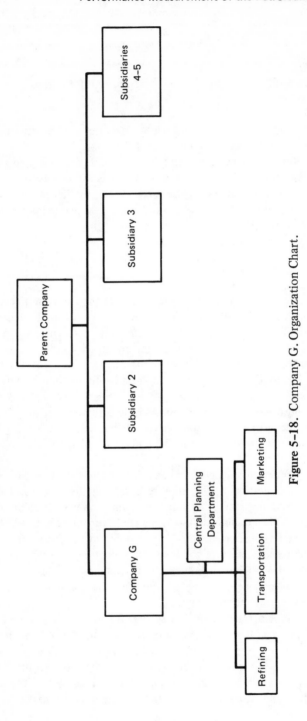

**Figure 5-18.** Company G. Organization Chart.

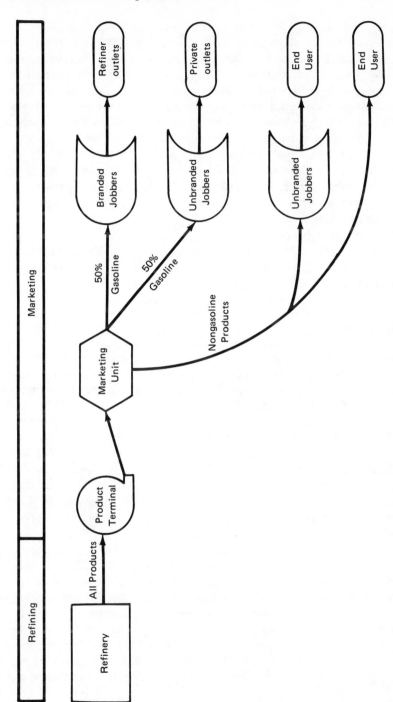

**Figure 5-19.** Company G. Product Distribution System

A complex computerized formula has been developed to generate transfer prices for a variety of products at different product terminals throughout the county. Basically, the system uses a combination of published prices and internally generated adjustments to arrive at an estimated product price. The starting point for developing the transfer price is a combination of published market prices. The published prices that are used represent sales from a product terminal (rack price). Analysts discount from the price the charges for transportation, financial credit or other service, and nonproduct charges, until they arrive at an estimate of the base price for the product at the Gulf Coast. The base price is then built back up again through adjustments until it represents the estimated price for the product in the quantity actually transferred from a refinery to the product terminal of the marketing function. The computed estimated price is the transfer price (figure 5-20).

Information that results from Company G's transfer pricing system is considered useful only for internal diagnostic purposes. No reports based on the transfer pricing system are given to anyone higher than the manager of Company G.

## Summary

This section discussed the need for performance measurement within the energy industry. Both the government and industry have turned increasingly to performance measurements as a means of monitoring more closely the industry's activities and achieving better management control.

This section showed the importance that the internal organization of a corporation plays in the evaluation of economic performance. Any data collection effort is influenced by the structure of the corporation supplying the data. Because structure varies by company and industry subsegment, the meaning of the data will also vary. Data will only be as consistent as the structure of the company and subsegment that supply them. Attempts to measure performance must take into consideration the nuances in the data, particularly financial data, resulting from different organizational structures.

The need for functional profitability, a key performance measure used by corporate managers, was discussed in terms of its applicability for evaluating segments of the petroleum industry. Functional profitability is a measure of profitability intended to indicate how effective corporate or business unit policies and decisions are in generating profits. The discussion focused on how functional profitability enhanced management control and resource allocation.

Also presented was a discussion of transfer prices, since they are necessary for calculating functional profitability. Transfer prices represent a connecting link between two business units. They supply information for decision-making

> Transfer Price = (Published rack price) – (Transportation costs) –
> (Credit charges) – (Service and other nonproduct
> charges) + (Transportation costs to refinery) +
> (Adjustments)

**Figure 5–20.** Company G. Gasoline Transfer Price Formula

and serve as a tool for evaluating a business unit's financial performance. Several methods for calculating transfer prices were presented. They include: cost-based, marginal cost, two-step, market price, negotiation, and linear programming. Contained in this section was a discussion of how corporations use any and all of these six methods for a variety of purposes, including resource allocation and management control. No method is perfect. Each meets the needs of some corporations in some circumstances. Special emphasis was placed on the need for management sensitivity to the potential problems of transfer pricing. Any business decision based on transfer pricing should be approached with extreme caution. For example, many oil companies that have spent twenty years developing sophisticated transfer pricing systems still use them for diagnostic rather than decision-making purposes.

Finally, this section discussed transfer pricing within the petroleum industry. The discussion is based on interviews that the authors had with eleven integrated oil companies. Oil companies design transfer pricing systems for developing internal data necessary for decision making. Like all data collection mechanisms, transfer pricing systems within the oil industry are viewed with a number of considerations in mind. First, they represent only one source of data. No company makes major operating decisions on the basis of one set of data. Each company continuously compares the results generated by a transfer pricing system with results based on other analytical tools. Second, the systems are normally designed for internal operating purposes. They assist with making decisions on internal activities ranging from diagnosing potential product line profitability problems to capital investments in the company. Finally, each company's system is tailored to meet the specific objectives for which it was designed. Using a transfer pricing system for a purpose other than the one for which it was designed may lead to unwarranted conclusions based on inappropriate data.

## Notes

1. Petroleum Industry Competition Act of 1976, "Report of the Committee on the Judiciary; United States Senate," June 28, 1976, p. 15.

2. Fred C. Allvine and James M. Patterson, *Competition, Ltd.* (Bloomington, Indiana University Press, 1972), p. 23.

3. Federal Energy Administration, Office of Regulatory Programs, *Final Report, Findings and Views Concerning the Mandatory Petroleum Allocation and Price Regulations,* September, 1977, p. 65.

4. Ibid.

# Part III
# An Economic Framework for Performance Evaluation

In part I, the principle was established that the term "performance evaluation" took on different meanings depending on the context in which it was applied. Various interest groups—managers, economists, regulators, stockholders, and competitors—have performance measurement problems, each of which are different.

This section presents an analysis of the performance measurement problem as seen by the economist. It is useful because economics is a subject that contributes positive explanations of the competitive behavior of firms and markets. Also, perhaps more significantly, economics serves as a basis for regulatory and competitive analysis.

Since the days of Adam Smith, economists have recognized the importance of economic gains and self-interest in promoting societal gains and public interest. The role of profits as an inducement to individuals to change the allocation of resources is central to economic theory.

Profits are not only the reward, but also the signal for undoing the temporary success. Profits are the signal for firms to enter or expand an industry. After expansion takes place, the socially efficient solution theoretically prevails. Firms in the industry would, in this long-run ideal position, earn no pure economic profits. With the sleight of hand of competition, the firms in the industry would be deceived. Society benefits from the condition of "no profits," but it would not attain such a position without the dynamics created by the pursuit of profit.

Classical economic theory is actually more refined than the story presented here. It is not really earned profits that induce entry, but rather the prospect of profits. Prospective profits can be distinguished from actual profits as follows:

1. Efficiency can lead to profits of both types. If inefficiency causes earned profits to be negative, prospective profits can still be positive, inducing entry by efficient firms.

2. Growth in sales may cause prospective profits to appear large despite current subpar earnings.

3. Imperfect information about the state of current earnings can lead to confusion about the prospects for future profits.

4. Prospective profits might never be converted into future earnings. The lack of spectacular earnings performance is not proof that prospective profits are insufficient to attract investment. It might be proof of vigorous competition.

5. Large current earnings might not reflect strong prospects for future earn-

ings. Indeed, the wise firm might recognize the stampede of entrants that would likely occur. Generally speaking, this situation will prevail only under unusual economic circumstances.

All of the generalizations drawn here are based on abstract concepts of equilibrium. The more general the problem to which these concepts are applied, the more useful they are. The more specific the problem, the more problems of realism become essential to a useful analysis.

General concepts of industry equilibrium are quite powerful in predicting the direction of changes in prices, output, and other industry variables in some unspecified time period known as the long-run. The precise dynamics of these variables are much more loosely understood. In fact, by the use of comparative statics the precise dynamics are ignored as long as they are stable, that is, as long as there is no reason to believe that along the time path from one static equilibrium point to another the equilibrium process will not go astray.

For the purposes of this book, it is most essential to understand that economic theory offers no generally acceptable foundation for predicting price levels and profits on even an annual basis with great accuracy. Absent a strong theoretical foundation, one cannot take the more difficult step of predicting annual prices and profits under comparative competitive conditions. Yet we can make strong comparative predictions about the equilibrium properties of alternative competitive states; we simply cannot do it with precision as to the absolute quantities. This deficiency is no deficiency at all given the purposes for which the theory was designed.

# 6 The Industrial Organization Paradigm

Faced with a changing industrial landscape, the economics profession has developed theories to explain industries characterized by monopoly, and monopolistic and oligopolistic competition. Various theories have also been developed to explain competition when firms are operated by professional managers rather than owner-entrepreneurs.

Modern-day additions to microeconomic theory are an eclectic group of tools. Faced with the desire to conduct empirical research, the profession has developed a general paradigm to be applied, albeit loosely, to all industrial organization research. This paradigm, articulated first by Edward Mason, depicts a set of theoretical relationships among the basic conditions, structure, conduct, and performance of an industry.[1] The discussion that follows draws on the general intellectual foundations of industrial organization.[2]

## Basic Conditions

The basic conditions of an industry are the factors influencing the supply and demand for the product. Examples of basic demand conditions are the price and income elasticity of demand and the degree to which the purchase of the product is complemented by the purchase of another product (such as automobiles and gasoline). Supply conditions include, for example, technological characteristics of the product and its production process.

## Market Structure

Structure refers to the degree to which competition is facilitated by the number and power of actors in the marketplace. There are three major elements of market structure: (1) concentration, (2) entry barriers, and (3) product differentiation.

The first element, concentration, offers a means of sizing up the degree to which competitors are interdependent, as opposed to being in a perfectly competitive market in which each firm has such a small market share as to be unconcerned about competitive reaction. The extreme values of concentration occur when either one firm dominates the market (has 100 percent of sales or production) or when many firms dominate such that each firm has an infinitesimal market share. The former situation would approximate monopoly and the latter perfect competition. Critics on both ends of the ideological spectrum would argue that concentration by itself is not a sufficient measure of monopoly power. Monopoly power and perfect competition each require a number of other facilitating factors.

Two observations are important to the purpose of this book. First, there is not a hypothesized continuous relationship between concentration variables and monopoly performance, however measured. One would expect large changes in concentration to be associated with changes in performance. However, a well-defined incremental relationship between small changes in the respective variables would not be expected. Second, there is no known threshold level of concentration above which oligopoly or monopoly power is predicted to exist.[3]

Concentration is typically measured by such variables as the combined market share (of sales, assets, employees, and production) of the $N$ largest sellers. Concentration measures are often supplemented by measures of asymmetry in the distribution of market shares as well as by measures of the turnover in the rankings of industry leaders. Together these measures provide a useful, if not complete, picture of an important dimension of competition.

In the petroleum industry, as in most others, there are several difficulties associated with computing and interpreting concentration levels. These include problems in defining the relevant product market (petroleum versus gasoline versus unleaded gasoline, for example); the relevant geographical market; and the relevant time frame for analysis.

Some recent data on concentration in the U.S. petroleum industry are displayed in table 6-1. Clearly, the levels of concentration do not portray a monopoly structure, nor do they suggest a market with no supplier more successful than others. A fact of life in the industry is that there are market share leaders. The concentration levels and trends in those values are certainly not the data to distinguish among efficiency and monopoly explanations for the sustained preeminence of the major firms.

Barriers to entry are useful variables to explain the past or predict the future with respect to entry of new competitors or expansion by existing competitors to pursue prospective profits.[4] Entry barriers affect performance in a dynamic sense, but they can have short-term effects on conduct and performance. When they are low, the potential for entry can be so strong as to limit the strategy and consequent performance of existing competitors. In that case, no structural change can be measured, yet barriers to entry would certainly have affected performance. When entry barriers are high, supranormal profits can be earned by existing firms with no threat of future profit erosion or structural change.

The most significant entry barrier in the petroleum industry is vertical integration. Because of its importance, it will be discussed separately. Three other

**Table 6-1**
**Concentration Ratios in the U.S. Petroleum Industry**

| Industry Segment | Shares of the Largest | |
|---|---|---|
| | Four Firms | Eight Firms |
| Petroleum refining (1972)[a] | 31.00 | 56.00 |
| Gasoline refining capacity (1970)[b] | 34.04 | 59.78 |
| Domestic crude oil production (net 1969)[b] | 31.09 | 50.54 |
| Lubrication oils and greases (1972)[a] | 31.00 | 44.00 |

[a]Source: *1972 Census of Manufacturers: Concentration Ratios in Manufacturing*, Washington, D.C., Department of Commerce, Bureau of Census.
[b]Source: *Preliminary FTC Staff Report of Its Investigation of the Petroleum Industry*, Washington, D.C., U.S. Federal Trade Commission, June 1973, tables II-1, II-2 and II-3.

alleged barriers to entry merit discussion: scale economies, absolute cost impediments, and product differentiation.

Barriers to entry resulting from economies of scale occur when firms within the industry must obtain a large market share before their unit costs fall to efficient levels. Such a situation in the marketplace confronts the new entrant with the requirement of building a large enough plant to capture lower costs at high volumes. At the same time, the new entrant must be certain that the new plant does not create overcapacity in the marketplace. Dealing with these two constraints provides the new entrant with no incentive to enter the marketplace, thereby reducing competitive forces. For the petroleum industry, however, there exist anomalies in the geographical distribution of demand, weak economies of scale, and small markets for certain products. These market characteristics provide many opportunities for new entry.[5]

Absolute cost levels represent the second type of barrier to entry. Absolute cost impediments exist when the costs of a new entrant will exceed those of existing firms within the market. Cost barriers result from many factors. Existing firms may have "locked up" the existing and easily accessible sources of crude reserves, skilled labor, or other critical factors of production. Also, capital costs may be lower for existing firms.

Large petroleum firms do realize lower capital costs, partially as a consequence of vertical integration. Since integration reduces risk and maximizes control, capital costs and profits should be lower. Capital costs follow levels of risk, while profits are inversely related to risk levels.

Lower capital costs for integrated companies do not necessarily imply the existence of barriers to entry, nor do low profit levels necessarily equate with inefficiency. The complex interrelationship of these market conditions does have implications for performance measurement and interpretation. The interrelationship underscores the need for properly analyzing the data. For example, the policy maker should not become immediately alarmed to find that profit rates of the nonintegrated oil company are higher than those of an integrated company. Companies that accept risky market opportunities in a competitive market are either rewarded by high profits if they succeed or are excluded from the marketplace if they fail. Concern would be appropriate if economic evidence indicated that the integrated company leveraged the control and lower capital costs that result from integration as a means to block the nonintegrated companies from seeking out and taking advantage of these opportunities.

Product differentiation results when consumers form different preferences among the individual brands of petroleum products. Product differentiation relates to market performance because it removes the pressure on oil companies within a market to sell at a single market price. In a market where product preference is expressed due to product differentiation, demand for the product is no longer based solely on price, but on a combination of price and perceived product characteristics. As a result, each oil company can set its own price policy (assuming no regulatory interference), and the form of price competition is changed.

Since we are dealing with commodities whose physical characteristics are similar among the various oil companies (heating oil, high octane gasoline, and regular gasoline), products are differentiated by means other than physical characteristics, such as conditions of sale. Various conditions of sale include credit arrangements, service support, terms of guarantee, and location of sale. The ability to influence these conditions of sale is enhanced when the product is sold through company stations.

Product differentiation has two important implications. First, it influences consumer demand for products. Consumers develop brand allegiances as a result of their preferences for the condition of sale. The second important implication of product differentiation is that it opens up new market strategies for the oil companies. Since demand for a product is more inelastic because of a strong brand preference, the company has a motivation to react to changes in market conditions by means other than price. The company now has a choice of changing price, credit service, or location of sale as a means of maintaining or increasing demand for the product.

The oil industry has been severely criticized for its expenditures on efforts to differentiate products. This criticism was particularly apparent during the course of legislative hearings for the Petroleum Industry Competition Act of 1976. During the course of these hearings, for example, several points clearly made were:

Sold under many brand names, gasoline is basically a fungible commodity. It consists of many chemically identifiable individual components that may be blended differently, yet product similar performance characteristics.

Companies routinely exchange gasoline, making it impossible to determine the original brand.

Additives are mass produced and sold by chemical firms to many different companies.

Consumers cannot make any appraisal of the difference in gasoline, aside from the brand preference created by advertising.

Improved analysis in the area of product differentiation is important for understanding the marketing segment. While product differentiation and its effects on the competitive process are difficult to quantify, there are guidelines that can be followed. These guidelines measure changes in the market resulting from efforts to differentiate products. The ability to track changes on a company basis and company category level over time related to price, advertising expenditures, credit services, and characteristics of service outlets is important.

## Market Conduct

The linkage between market structure (opportunity) and performance (motive) in any industry is the conduct it chooses to implement (the modus operandi). Conduct is usefully divided into two types: policies towards the market and policies toward rivals.[6] The most important aspect of conduct is price, but other aspects such as product quality, distribution practices, and advertising are also important.

An important group of conduct patterns centers around determining oligopolistic market prices, that is, the way in which firms set their prices and change them in response to others.[7] Companies use a variety of approaches in setting prices, including targeted ROI, standard markup added to cost, and incremental pricing.[8] They often make these pricing decisions in anticipation of rivals' reactions. Prices for the integrated company are also set in light of the issue of control. Control for an integrated company is critical to the efficient allocation of its resources and, hence, its performance. An integrated company could sacrifice beneficial price decisions for better control because, in the long-run, control results in more efficient resource allocations. The oil industry's capital intensiveness demands this tight level of control because it means a secure raw material supply (crude) and assured outlets for products (markets). This premium on control has price implications. For instance, the most secure crude may not be, and frequently is not, the least expensive. On the marketing side, company-owned stations may not be the most profitable channels of distribution, but they are a secure channel.

In the domestic oil industry, pricing policies and, hence, conduct, are determined as much by governmental policies as by market forces. Governmental intervention has been systematic and comprehensive, ranging from policies designed to stimulate production to policies that attempt to control output to support crude oil prices.[9]

Duchesneau provides a clear summary of how government regulations have affected market conduct in the petroleum industry.[10] He states that competition in the industry has been systematically reduced by governmental intervention. Restrictions on oil imports and demand prorationing have had anticompetitive effects on conduct. These regulations have resulted in patterns of company conduct that private monopoly would have pursued if it had the necessary capability.

Some patterns of conduct involve strategies to affect market structure. These patterns of conduct are coercive because they worsen the structural position of some business rivals. Coercive conduct generally cuts in one or both of two directions: (1) taming, weakening, or eliminating existing business rivals; and (2) raising the barriers to entry to curtail the supply of potential rivals.[11] In both cases, inefficient allocation results. Coercive actions can take place only in markets where concentration is high enough so that each firm is affected by the conduct of any rival.

Vertical integration has been alleged to be a coercive practice, based on the belief that integration facilitates oligopolistic coordination. By possessing the ability to "squeeze" nonintegrated rivals through raising the price of upstream products, oil companies can exert coercive discipline. This is not the usual predatory pricing argument, since petroleum companies do not have a monopoly position at any stage. The arguments related to vertical integration are discussed further in chapter 7.

This is not the forum for determining if coercive practices do or do not exist in the industry. Sufficient economic analysis exists and has been cited to show that coercive policies have not been effective, whether they have been attempted or not. John M. Blair notes that, despite the impressive advantages of integration, the majors began during the mid 1960s to suffer a steady deterioration in their domestic earnings.[12]

## Market Performance

Performance, in the most simplified sense, is the "bottom line" of competition. The most obvious measures of performance from private and public perspectives are profits and efficiency. In a dynamic capital-intensive industry such as petroleum, technological progressiveness is a third dimension of performance.

Besides its function as a gauge of market operationability, performance is part of a larger, dynamic process. The level of performance realized can affect conduct and structure. Conduct can either be reinforced or revealed to be erroneous and, therefore, altered. In closing the information gap between expec-

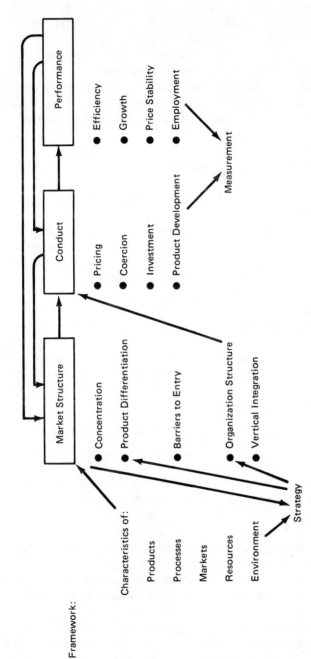

**Figure 6–1.** Dynamic Relationship of Structure, Conduct, and Performance

tations and realizations about performance, expectations can be adjusted. Also, through differences in performance among existing competitors, particularly through exit of failing firms, structure may also be altered.

Figure 6-1 illustrates the dynamic relationships just described. The primary line of causation runs from basic conditions to market structure to conduct to performance. The feedback flows are displayed along the top of the figure. At any point in time, this simultaneous system could be observed, but without true meaning. Only over time do the rigorous forces exhibit themselves.

## Measuring the Usefulness of Performance Measures

Having outlined an economic framework for assessing the vigor of competition in the petroleum industry, it is now possible to present an economic analysis of the potential usefulness of various performance measures. The comments on each type of measure reflect the dynamic role of performance in economic theory in general, and industrial organization in particular. They also reflect some realities about the nature of the petroleum industry.

### Corporate-Wide Profitability

Ideally, economic performance analysis should be conducted with economic data. When economic data are not available, accounting data must be substituted. The limitations of accounting data as proxy for economic data are particularly evident with regard to profits.[13] Some limitations are:

a.  Accounting profits are short-term records (annual and quarterly) of past results; the most relevant profit measure for economic analysis is prospective profit.
b.  Accounting profits are affected by the business cycle, whereas prospective profits are related to a different (future) phase of the cycle.
c.  Periodic and large investments are depreciated according to accounting conventions that do not reflect the current value of assets.
d.  Such expenditures as advertising and research and development are not always capitalized, thereby lowering reported profits.
e.  The current value of assets, such as replacement cost, is not attributed to equity. Return on equity is, therefore, an overstatement of profitability.

Recognition of profits yields some obvious intricacies. High reported profits could be caused by high revenues from market power, low costs, or a combination of both. Likewise, low reported profits could be caused by low revenues due to strong competition, high costs due to poor efficiency, or a combination of both. Research by economists has long been plagued by the inadequacy of data for testing economic hypotheses, such as the relationship between industry concentration and profitability.

Chapter 3 described the problems associated with determining the profitability of individual functional segments. Neither cost allocations nor transfer prices are required when measuring profits on a corporate-wide basis. Profitability measurements that can be applied on a corporate-wide basis are those discussed earlier: profits (before and after tax), ROI, and cash-flow analysis. These do not exhaust the variations on the basic profit calculation, but represent the major useful profit measures.

Corporations in the oil industry view their operations in terms of long-range opportunities and costs. The need for long-term planning stems from the large financial commitments required in a capital-intensive industry. Returns from large capital investments are received over a period of years. Therefore, evaluation of the results of corporate activities are also viewed from the long-term perspective by oil companies.

Data analysis should also reflect this emphasis on trends. The changes in patterns of profitability—among groups of firms of different size, regional market emphasis, degree of vertical integration, and extent of diversification— provide better insights into the economic performance of the oil industry than snapshot views at the end of a given year. Used in this manner, measures of corporate-wide profitability can be linked with other measures described here to address some of the policy questions in the industry.

No individual measure is perfect, but a combination of measures can be used to deduce true relationships. The structure, conduct, and performance model is a good vehicle for analysis.

For example, a key question when monitoring the economic performance of the energy industry is the impact that changes in concentration have on corporate profits. To determine this, it is necessary to look at the linkage between structure (concentration), conduct, and performance (corporate-wide profits).

If increased industry concentration were to occur simultaneously with increased profits, it could be hypothesized that greater efficiencies have resulted in lower costs, or that greater concentration has afforded the opportunities for oligopolistic pricing.

Conduct measures can be employed to distinguish between the two alternatives. Comparing cost data over time and among companies, the efficiency arguments can be examined. Data on prices can be explored to evaluate the hypothesized pricing practices. This is one example of how performance measures applied to the structure, conduct, and performance model can provide clues to the performance of the industry.

*Prices*

The general level of prices, whether ex-refinery or at the retail level, is too broad for gauging economic performance. Alfred Marshall long ago dispelled the myth that there exists some "normal" competitive price. However, the changes over time of prices can be employed in forming testable hypotheses. For example, a downward trend in prices not justified by lowered costs could indicate predatory pricing behavior. The published price series discussed in chapter 8 are one source of information. This information is only an estimate, because selling prices of internal transfers should be compared to sales to independent companies. To complicate matters, the value of such a comparison—of transfer prices to third party sales—is questionable.

Using the differences in price among buyers as a performance measure is very difficult. Buyers pay different prices partly because the nature of the product is different. What is purchased is not just a refined product, but also terms of payment, (in some cases) a brand name, wholesaling services, assurances of supply (long-term contracts versus spot sales), among many other product attributes affecting the price of any transaction.[14] Even if the various factors affecting price were accounted for, differences among prices to independents and internal transfer prices would not offer conclusive evidence of the existence of a "squeeze" on independents.

The economics of vertical integration is too complex to allow such rapid conclusions to be drawn, as will be demonstrated.

A simple financial reporting system cannot substitute for special-purpose evidentiary studies. Given the difficulties of satisfactorily removing the influence of many complicating factors, reported price data appear unlikely to contribute positively even to the formation of preliminary hypotheses.

*Costs*

A variety of cost measures appear relevant for understanding the efficiencies and motivations of petroleum companies. Production costs by product, vertical function, and location would contribute usefully to understanding the industry. To understand the usefulness and limitations of such data, a series of economic issues requires discussion. First, product costs by product by region are inadequate for understanding efficiency. Transportation costs (of refined product) are important too. The higher the transportation costs, the more sensible is geographical dispersion of smaller refineries to points closer to end-use markets at a sacrifice of higher unit production costs.[15] Such spatial factors, complicated further by the dynamics of capacity expansion, render simple comparisons of production costs in different regions inadequate. The existing constellation of refineries is largely a function of historical incentives, as well as other factors such as crude pipeline locations. The production costs in those refineries are determined by the incentive to minimize costs in the multiplant system. The individual plant costs taken alone make little sense.[16]

A complication in understanding differences in costs (and therefore profits) among products is the joint cost problem. The refining process produces products jointly. While accounting techniques exist for separating costs by product, these distinctions are purely arbitrary. For example, heavy fuel oil once sold at a price less than crude oil. Could this have been profitable? As long as incremental cost was below the price, it was profitable.

> Refining a ton of crude oil is profitable, and will be done if the receipts cover the *total* costs of the operation, including the necessary profit, while no *individual* product will be forthcoming if the market price is above its incremental cost.[17]

One cost distinction that can be addressed is plant-specific versus product-specific costs. Product-specific costs are directly associated with the production of a specific product. While the joint cost problem in petroleum is still a problem, at least the unit costs associated with increasing output with a given product mix can be obtained. Plant-specific costs are associated with increasing plant output, regardless of which products are involved. Such items as shipping, administration, maintenance, and other overhead functions belong in the plant-specific category. By properly distinguishing between plant- and product-specific costs, economic analysis can be facilitated.

*Capacity and Capacity Utilization*

Capacity and capacity utilization data could be valuable for policy analysis. First, investment adequacy is itself a measure of industry performance. How the market at any stage performs over time, a dynamic efficiency criterion, is largely determined by investment behavior.[18] One difficulty in such an assessment is the fact that investment decisions are made in an *ex ante* environment, while performance measurement would be done *ex post*. That the long-run efficiency of markets is poorly understood is reflected in the following:

> But resource markets may be rather vulnerable to surprises. They may respond to shocks about the volume of reserves, or about competition from new materials, or about the costs of competing technologies, or even about near-term political events, by drastic movements of current price and production. It may be quite a while before the transvaluation of values . . . settle down under the control of sober future prospects. In between it may be a hard winter.[19]

Using uncertainties about prices and quantities as an explanation for market failure is a circular argument, though not necessarily a fallacy.

That is, if all markets for future goods existed and cleared all transactions, then there would be no price-quantity uncertainties. But this
much is true: if some markets for future goods do not exist, then the
agents have uncertainties which are relevant to their behavior on markets for complementarity and substitution can occur over time as well
as simultaneously. If . . . uncertainty can tend to destroy markets, then
we can conclude that the absence of some markets for future goods
may cause others to fail.[20]

Given the absence of a norm, in economic theory, for ideal investment behavior over time, the value of *ex post* analysis of *ex ante* behavior is somewhat
tenuous. It is not obvious how investment ought to behave in a competitive
market. The presence of risk and the absence of (or inefficiencies in using)
futures markets, are in fact, incentives for vertical integration in petroleum.
But, a comparison of investment (and other) performance of the vertically integrated versus nonvertically integrated firms might just be a comparison of market segments that coexist *because* of the differences in performance being
investigated. If that is the case, it would be no great revelation, nor would it
imply an absence of the vigor of competition.

A second use of capacity data would be in testing the rationality of capacity
growth. The existence of positive investment in a segment where reported profits
are negative or substandard could be a sign of predation, cross-subsidization, or
poor management. More likely, it would be a reflection of poor profit data, institutional or regulatory incentives, a distorted static snapshot of a dynamic process, or a partial analysis of a more complex logistical management process.
However, in forming preliminary testable hypotheses, such analysis could be
useful. If the data were used to draw unsupported, simplistic policy conclusions,
they would be harmful.

A third use of capacity data would be to test whether vertically integrated
firms do have higher capacity utilization, as alleged by industry proponents.

A fourth use would be in testing for the existence of a capital bias in regulated industries.[21] Are capacity costs growing more rapidly than desirable due to
their being added to the rate base?

A fifth use of capacity data would be in testing the "excess capacity in
marketing" thesis. Perhaps such excess capacity might be a sign of preemption of
markets to deter new entry. But it would also be a sure sign of monopolistic
competition, a reasonable description of gasoline marketing competition.[22]

## Exchanges

The exchange of crude oil and refined products among companies is an interesting measure. Exchanges are undertaken as a way to minimize transportation
costs and circumvent the restrictions of geographical plant size limitations.[23]

They are also a coordinating device, whereby companies obtain insights into the prices, capacity, and future plans of their competitor. An exchange, therefore, can be efficient and also contribute to oligopolistic coordination.

The terms under which exchanges are effected are interesting. Along with internal transfers and sales to independents, they complete the sales picture. For that reason, it would be helpful to understand the terms at which exchanges take place, wherever possible.

*Research and Development*

Expenditures on research and development, broken out by vertical function where possible, would be another interesting measure of performance. Although the measurement of this dimension of industry performance (usually seen as a proxy for technological progressiveness) through inputs, that is, expenditures, rather than outputs is imperfect, there is no choice.

**Summary**

The structure-conduct-performance paradigm has been offered as a better lens through which to view the petroleum industry. Corporate-wide profitability combined with measures not related to profits can help government officials begin to address performance issues. These performance measures supplemented with the elements of structure and patterns of behavior discussed in this study fit together to assist in the evaluation of the oil industry's performance, obviating the need for functional profitability. As Kaysen and Turner have pointed out, the ideal analysis would flow from market structure to processes to performance.

> We would then be able both to deduce present performance from obser-
> vation of present structure, and to predict what alterations in per-
> formance would result from particular changes in structure. Further,
> we would be able to say to what extent any observed pattern of per-
> formance was compelled by the structure of the market, and to what
> extent it was the result of policy choices by firms, which could well
> have been other than they were."[24]

Unfortunately, even the economic framework described in this study can neither "predict market performance from market structure, nor [can it] tell from structure alone how competitive the processes of the market are."[25]

Although a large literature exists on the subject of employing the model,[26] there exists also formidable methodological and data problems that render empirical tests of the model far from conclusive.[27] One test of the structure-conduct-performance model in explaining the performance of the petroleum refining industry has yielded reasonably good relationships among structural, conduct, and performance variables.[28] This study might conceivably serve as background for analysis done with data collected in the FRS.

Why then is the structure-conduct-performance model offered at all? The answer is not because more or better data will allow the estimation of clean relationships. Rather, it is because the scarce commodity in evaluating petroleum industry performance is a tolerance for complexity and ambiguity, rather than a scarcity of data. Since the structure-conduct-performance model offers a thought process for formulating more useful hypotheses than does simple profit analysis, and can make some order out of statistical chaos, it offers promise. On the other hand, since the extent of vertical integration and capital intensity makes the petroleum industry unique, the state of current industrial organization knowledge should not define the limits of fruitful hypothesis formulation.

One of the weaknesses of industrial organization to date has been "a disposition to search for monopolistic explanations for all business practices whose justification is not obvious to the meanest intelligence.[29] At the other extreme are industry points of view that rationalize all economic phenomena as stemming from efficiency.

What is needed is (1) an explicit delineation of all competing hypotheses from industrial organization, tempered by the realities of the petroleum industry, and (2) data that will offer evidence to support or refute the hypotheses.

The complexity of petroleum industry economics and the ambiguity of performance measures are facts of life that cannot be altered simply by collecting more data. But by continuous monitoring of the dynamic relationships of structure, conduct, and performance, one can begin to understand if the petroleum industry is behaving in a competitive nature that is the most appropriate for the American economy.

## Notes

1. E. Mason, "Price and Production Policies of Large-Scale Enterprise," *American Economic Review,* Supplement, March 1939, pp. 61–74, and "The Current State of the Monopoly Problem in the United States," *Harvard Law Review,* June 1949, pp. 1265–1285.

2. See, e.g., F.M. Scherer, *Industrial Market Structure and Economic Performance* (Chicago, Rand McNally, 1970).

3. See J.W. Meehan, Jr. and T. Duchesneau, "The Critical Level of Concentration: An Empirical Analysis," *Journal of Industrial Economics,* vol. 22, September 1973, for a conclusion to the contrary.

4. A classic work on entry barriers is by J.S. Bain, *Barriers to New Competition,* (Cambridge, Harvard University Press, 1956).

5. Evidence to support this can be found in F.M. Scherer, A.R. Becken-

stein, E. Kaufer, and R.D. Murphy, *The Economics of Multi-Plant Operation: An International Comparisons Study,* (Cambridge, Harvard University Press, 1975), cited hereafter as SBKM.

6. R. Caves, *American Industry: Structure, Conduct, Performance,* fourth edition (Englewood Cliffs, N.J., Prentice-Hall, Inc., 1977), p. 50.

7. Ibid., p. 65.

8. As reported in J.M. Blair, *Control of Oil* (New York, Pantheon Books, 1976).

9. See U.S. Senate, Subcommittee on Antitrust and Monopoly, *Government Intervention in the Market Place,* Washington, D.C., 1969.

10. T.D. Duchesneau, *Competition in the U.S. Energy Industry* (Cambridge, Ballinger Publishing, 1975).

11. Caves, *American Industry,* p. 63.

12. Blair, *Control of Oil,* p. 241.

13. This section draws on observations made in Scherer, *Industrial Market Structure.*

14. The recognition of "brand" as a relevant product attribute was offered in *Borden Co.* vs. *Federal Trade Commission,* 381 F.2d 175 (1967), a price discrimination case.

The FTC offered a messy treatment of section 2(c) of the Robinson-Patman Act, relating to the offering of brokerage commissions or discounts in lieu of brokerage services, in *FTC* vs. *Standard Oil Co. of Indiana et al.,* 355 U.S. 396 (1958).

15. See the discussion of the evidence of the SBKM study, *The Economics of Multi-Plant Operation.*

16. Ibid., p. 655. An example (for glass bottle industry) was cited where a multiplant, multiproduct firm operated at a minimum total (production-plus-transport) cost, yet a number of plants produced products at cost sacrifices relative to a minimum optimal scale output level. This illustrates the dangers of making simple cost analyses.

17. M. Adelman, *The World Petroleum Market* (Baltimore, Johns Hopkins University Press, 1972), p. 175.

18. See J.M. Clark, *Competition as a Dynamic Process* (Washington, D.C., Brookings, 1961) for a good discussion of the dynamics of market competition.

19. R.M. Solow, "The Economics of Resources or the Resource of Economics," *American Economic Review,* vol. 64, no. 2, May 1974, p. 7.

20. K. Arrow, "Limited Knowledge and Economic Analysis," *American Economic Review,* vol. 64, no. 1, March 1974, p. 9.

21. The well-known "A-J Effect," described in H. Averch and L. Johnson, "Behavior of the Firm Under Regulatory Constraint," *American Economic Review,* vol. 52, December, 1962, pp. 1053–69, is the bias in question.

22. In the sense of E.H. Chamberlin, *The Theory of Monopolistic Competition* (Cambridge, Harvard University Press, 1933).

23. The SBKM study, *The Economics of Multi-Plant Operation,* uncovered the common usage of such arrangements in the refining segment.

24. C. Kaysen and D.F. Turner, *Antitrust Policy: An Economic and Legal Analysis* (Cambridge, Harvard University Press, 1959), p. 60.

25. Ibid., p. 61.

26. See H. Goldschmid, et al., *Industrial Concentration: The New Learning* (Boston, Little Brown, 1974), for a very complete set of articles on the topic.

27. See L. Weiss, "Quantitative Studies of Industrial Organization," in *Frontiers of Quantitative Economics,* M.D. Intrilligator, ed. (Amsterdam, North Holland, 1971), for a good summary of the evidence.

28. H.L. Gabel, "A Simultaneous Equation Analysis of Industrial Structure and Performance," unpublished dissertation, University of Pennsylvania, 1977.

29. R. Coase, "Industrial Organization: A Proposal for Research," in *Policy Issues and Research Opportunities in Industrial Organization,* V.R. Fuchs, ed. (New York, Columbia University Press, 1972).

# 7 The Economics of Vertical Integration

Vertical integration is a predominant feature in the oil industry. Because of vertical integration's central position in economic arguments related to the petroleum industry, it is discussed in detail here. This section reviews the history of vertical integration and its relationship to government regulations, business strategy, and anticompetitive behavior.

One of our purposes is to allow competitive analysis of the petroleum industry. Another is to assess the impact of regulatory actions on competition and performance. Examining the economics of vertical integration offers insights into the potential usefulness of performance evaluation. Moreover, economic forces historically have influenced the organization structure as much as business considerations such as planning and control. Competition and the desire (not necessarily requited) to suppress competition have been important in determining business structure.

## Historical Development of Integration

John D. Rockefeller's Standard Oil Company led the early development of vertical integration in the petroleum industry. A strategy of aggressive pricing—the Court determined that the pricing was predatory,[1] but subsequent analysis has cast doubt on that conclusion[2]—and subsequent acquisition of weakened rivals' refining capacity, combined with the extraction of favorable and exclusionary rail rates, allowed Standard Oil Company to acquire a monopoly position in refining, crude oil transportation, and various segments of marketing.

The buildup of integration occurred first in the transportation/refining link. First through railroads and then through pipelines, Standard Oil Company established increased control of transportation facilities, which solidified its ability to gain control of the refining segment. With the discovery of the Gulf Coast oil fields at the turn of the century,

> the new, well-financed firms . . . made significant inroads on [Standard's] preeminent position. . . . Standard's share of the industry's rated daily crude refinery capacity fell from 82 percent in 1899 to 64 percent in 1911.[3]

The downstream integration from production to refining by the newcomers (including Gulf and Texaco) was a competitive threat, although not a dominant one, to Standard's refining and marketing control.

The dissolution of the Standard Oil Company was the major cause of structural change in the industry in this century. The new companies created out of the dissolution of the Standard Oil Company were largely integrated refiners and marketers. This was "in an era when a major new market for gasoline was being created by a widespread and rapidly-growing automobile market, reinforced early in the period by additional demands for petroleum products generated by World War I."[4]

The new, fragmented refining structure meant that the downstream operations were at the mercy of the booms and busts of the production of crude. For efficiency-related reasons, such as risk reduction, higher capacity utilization through coordinated throughput planning, scale economies, and capital raising, the now-competitive industry was forced to integrate backward to survive.

The nature of vertical integration in the petroleum industry changed dramatically in the late 1920s and early 1930s with discoveries of large oil reserves in East Texas and the Persian Gulf. Two important attributes of these discoveries—low cost, high-profit crude, and the true internationalization of the industry—dominated the vertical structure of the industry from that point until the present.

Adelman argues that the key to understanding the rationale for integration downstream is the existence of low cost, high-profit crude oil. To protect crude profits, final product prices must be protected. Yet the refining and marketing segments are more regional in character. They are also easier to enter. Given such heightened competition relative to crude oil, profits are predictably lower at downstream stages. If competition erodes prices in final markets through erosion at either the refining or marketing stages, the value of crude oil is lowered. "The integrated producer-refiner will indeed be more cautious about cutting refined prices in any one place, because if the reduction spreads, he will be more heavily penalized for it than will an independent local refiner."[5]

Therefore, to protect profits, the large crude producers integrated downstream. But, with subsequent rapid growth in consumption and the recent tightening of crude profits, the control of the integrated majors was lessened.

**Vertical Integration and Government Regulations**

Another issue related to vertical integration was the oil depletion allowance. The depletion allowance, when it was fully in effect, was alleged to create incentives for pricing crude oil higher.[6] This would supposedly give the integrated firms an advantage. The allowance permitted producers to deduct from their taxable income a fixed percentage of the value of oil. By showing profits at the crude oil stage, where the tax rate was lower due to the depletion allowance, the taxes for an integrated firm could be reduced. Richard Mancke has demonstrated that this would have been advantageous only if a company were at least 93 percent self-sufficient in crude oil, a condition that excluded many of the majors in recent years.[7] If, however, an individual corporate decision were undertaken only internally (in transfer prices between producing subsidiaries and refining subsidiaries), there is no reason to believe that the corporation would (or could) worry about the impact on externally purchased crude prices.

With the industry becoming truly multinational, institutional incentives to price crude oil higher in countries with lower tax rates were deemed an important influence on crude prices to U.S. refineries and, therefore, an influence on the ability of independent refiners to compete with integrated firms. The movement of crude and products through an integrated company is accomplished by transfer pricing.[8] Adelman, in questioning the logic of the relevance of tax-minimizing transfer prices to real competitive prices, offers the following:

> Transfer prices from one to another division of the same corporate entity are simply bookkeeping notations to permit the corporation to minimize its total tax bill. There is no market without independence or freedom to bargain. No market, no price. Hence, posted "prices" and intracorporate "prices" need detain us only the few moments necessary to suggest why anyone takes them seriously.[9]

Carrying this argument further, Adelman adds: "Since over four-fifths of oil output moves through integrated channels, there is no *necessary* relationship between the arm's-length crude price and the crude equivalent of what is finally realized from the sale of refined products."[10]

The events of the early 1970s drastically changed the environment in which the petroleum industry operates. Oil prices were controlled; tariffs and taxes were levied; and profits have been passed increasingly to OPEC. Additionally, extensive regulation has been imposed on the industry. The magnitude of change may alter the current vertical structure of the industry.

### The Economics of Vertical Integration in the Petroleum Industry

A review of the economic hypotheses about vertical integration is necessary to evaluate the potential usefulness of data assessing various competitive hypotheses. Additional arguments made to support vertically integrated petroleum companies are related to efficiency. Two major approaches have been taken in efficiency studies: transactions costs and scale economies.

#### Transaction Costs

The transactions cost literature is primarily the work of Oliver Williamson[11] and applied to petroleum by David Teece.[12] By focusing on the costs of market contracting and comparing them to the costs of long-term contracts and the costs of internal organization, one can reach an understanding of the efficiencies of vertical integration. According to Teece:

> . . . the requisite contracts for crude oil, R&D services, product supply, and so forth, cannot be written, executed or enforced. This paper demonstrates that supply and demand uncertainty, the capital intensive character of many industry investments, and the opportunistic proclivities of human decision makers renders it prudent for firms to integrate across particular stages of industry activity. The resultant vertically integrated firm is able to adapt to changing economic circumstances more efficiently, to attenuate opportunism more efficiently, to coordinate complementary investments more exactly, and to schedule production and inventories more efficiently.[13]

Teece's work offers insights into dealing with markets that are stochastic and dynamic, risky, and suffer from incomplete information. In short, he deals with all the elements of markets that form the basis for competition in the vertically integrated petroleum industry. Teece's work is relevant to the task of evaluating long-term performance in petroleum markets. That the long-term performance of markets is most relevant, but commonly ignored by conventional economics, is a fact that has been cited by masters in economic theory. Alfred Marshall notes:

> The element of time is a chief cause of these difficulties in economic investigation which make it necessary for man with his limited powers to go step by step; breaking up a complex question. . . . In breaking it up, he segregates those disturbing causes, whose wanderings happen to be inconvenient, for the time in a pound called Caeteris Paribus. . . . The more the issue is thus narrowed, the more exactly it can be handled; but also the less closely does it correspond to real life.[14]

Kenneth Arrow[15] and others[16] have addressed the lack of futures markets as an obstacle in applying economic theory to questions of the dynamic equilibrium behavior of markets. These futures markets fail to arise, Arrow alleges, due to uncertainty about the future, and the large cost of enforcing forward contracts. Both conditions clearly apply to the petroleum industry, and it would seem that the Williamson-Teece analysis views the strategy of vertical integration as an affirmative correction for the failures of vertical markets. That economic theory fails to address the very issues that motivate the long-run behavior of petroleum companies is the central paradox that needs to be understood before evaluating the potential usefulness of performance data.

On the topic of integration between refining and marketing, Teece offers the following conclusions:

Refiners integrated into the marketing to ensure quality service (as the service station replaced the general store) and to provide a window into the market place.

The nonconvergence of expectations between refiners (who wanted to expand supply) and independent dealers (who were unsure of the appropriate number and location of outlets) led to forward integration. This was especially true in situations where large product pipelines were being developed.

Backward integration by marketers was induced by supply uncertainties.

The "great volumetric interdependence in the industry, the huge throughput relative to inventory capacity, and the high costs of inventories relative to refining margins" all favor integration.[17]

## Scale Economies

There are definite similarities in substance, if not approach, between Teece's work and scale economy studies. A study of scale economies and the economics of multiplant operation, including petroleum refining, was published by Scherer, Beckenstein, Kaufer and Murphy (SBKM) in 1975.[18] Some of their results apply directly to an analysis of vertical integration.

SBKM found the minimum optimal scale (MOS) of refinery to be 200,000 barrels per day of crude oil processing capacity, with a one-third-of-MOS-sized refinery suffering a 4.8 percent elevation in unit costs. The advantages of operating a multiplant system, the further consequences of which would be vertical integration, were seen to offer few strategic advantages in geographical and product specialization relative to the single-plant refiner.[19] Slight advantages were found in terms of peak spreading, risk spreading and other massed reserves, research and development, and advertising and image differentiation. Moderate advantages were found in the cost of acquiring capital, mostly based on large firm size advantages.

The SBKM study discovered that multirefinery operations had slight to moderate advantages over a single refinery operations in terms of efficiently expanding capacity.[20] Why cannot a market be employed to confer these advantages on all refiners? "Securing all potentially attainable scale economies through market transactions linked to investment decisions may be both impractical and socially unpalatable."[21]

On the topic of vertical integration backward to achieve "least common multiple" combinations of plants, each operating at MOS volumes along a vertical chain, SBKM found moderate advantages to the larger multiplant firm. These advantages stem largely from the ability of the larger refiners to minimize risk in crude supplies by diversification of sources.

SBKM found little evidence of foreclosure of channels of distribution to independent, nonintegrated refiners, indicating there may be no relationship between vertical integration and access to distribution channels. In addition, the regional, single-plant refiner has had little trouble integrating downstream when it was deemed desirable.[22]

Since policy analysts are concerned with the existence of small, nonintegrated petroleum companies, it is important to ask what the implications are of the SBKM study with respect to small-operator opportunities. Only by understanding how small operations find survival opportunities can we make informed analyses of the impact of large company actions on small company performance.

Beckenstein[23] criticized the notion of comparing costs of small companies (or plants) to those of large companies to understand the viability of small enterprise, and goes on to conclude that,

> due to factors such as high transport costs, anomalies in the geographic distribution of demand, weak economies of scale, small markets for certain products . . . there will be various and sundry opportunities for small business.[24]

Some of these conditions apply to the petroleum industry. As such, complex interactions of phenomena provide small business opportunities in petroleum. These independents may or may not be integrated.

One example is the Shallow Water Refining Company, which operated a profitable 3,000 barrel per day refinery in western Kansas at a profit based on a geographical advantage.[25] In Shallow Water's case, and in the case of most small company opportunities, the data one could collect on the costs, prices, and profits of integrated competitors versus those of the small competitor would offer little insight into the true competitive picture. That these opportunities prosper or dwindle has little to do with the vertical integration.

As demonstrated by Edward Mitchell, large vertically integrated petroleum companies probably realize lower capital costs than other firms.[26] Mitchell found that vertical integration reduces business risk and, therefore, capital costs. He discovered that refiners improve stock ratings by integrating backward up to 50 percent crude self-sufficiency. Also, integration downstream into product pipelines improves stock ratings.

## Vertical Integration and Business Strategy

The key to understanding vertical integration as it fits into oil company business strategy is control. Oil is not the only industry where control is important. However, the oil industry is the most capital intensive of all industries. According to the May 1978 issue of *Fortune,* of the 500 largest industrial companies in the United States, the top ten firms in terms of assets per employee consisted of nine oil companies and one petrochemical firm. Because of oil's capital intensiveness, control is perceived to be of crucial importance. Control, in the context of the petroleum industry, means a secure and inexpensive raw material supply (crude) and assured outlets for products (markets). There are several conflicts apparent in some aspects of integration. For instance, the most secure crude may not be, and frequently is not, the least expensive. On the marketing side, company-owned stations may not be the most profitable channels of distribution.

If markets operated perfectly, there would be no need for vertical integration. Markets, of course, do not operate perfectly and, in the eyes of the oil industry, there is a need for vertical integration. The intermediate step—between the perfect markets and integration—is short or long-term contracts. While they do play a role and were more significant in the industry's early decades than they presently are, they are judged to be insufficient in reducing uncertainties. To assume as much control as is justifiable over all phases of operations is the objective. The vehicle through which this control is exercised is vertical integration.

The oil industry has been characterized at various times as being an industry that goes from "feast to famine."[27] This is because of the very capital intensiveness of the energy sector where full capacity utilization means profit and idle capacity means inadequate return. Therefore, since the investments that have to be made are very large, investors have undertaken them with that assurance of control that only vertical integration could provide. Recent results affirm the soundness of such a strategy. Gabel found evidence supporting the claim of McLean and Haigh that vertically integrated firms do have higher refining capacity utilization than nonintegrated firms.[28]

The size of investments that the oil industry has to make emphasizes the need for planning. The Trans-Arabian pipeline in the 1950s, Alaskan pipeline in the 1960s and 1970s, and the North Sea in the 1970s are obvious examples. Planning requires information and knowledge, and the industry has used the various phases of an integrated operation to keep up and to improve the informational flow within one corporate umbrella. Moreover, since the size of the investments is so huge, vertically integrated firms manage to coordinate them through the different phases of the integration operations. Oil companies now require significant outside financing. Their debt/equity ratios have doubled in the last ten years. Every time the major companies enter the capital markets, the size of the financing is so large that the lifetime of the project—in changing environments—is under control. This adds yet another argument, in the eyes of the industry, for vertical integration.

With the major oil companies pursuing control and efficiency objectives through integration, there remain segments of the market where nonintegrated independents can and should exist. The integrated major finds itself unable to manage both the normal business and the opportunistic niches in the market-place. As such, the industry takes on a dual structure: the majors and the inde-pendents. Each exists for different purposes and, therefore, performs differently. This process is a function of the same competitive force as it interacts with the institutional realities of operating a corporation.

### Vertical Integration and Potential Anticompetitive Behavior

Having considered the efficiency arguments surrounding vertical integration and petroleum industry economics, the arguments alleging anticompetitive behavior through vertical integration must be considered. The most common argument states that widespread vertical integration in petroleum facilitates oligopolistic coordination. By possessing the ability to squeeze nonintegrated rivals through raising the price of upstream products, oligopolistic discipline is easier to exert. This is not the usual predatory pricing argument, since petroleum companies have no monopoly position at any stage with the possible exception of pipelines, which are regulated. It is instead an argument that the recognition of mutually beneficial strategies (through parallel behavior) is enhanced by vertical integra-tion. More important, competitive urges to follow individual motivations, rather than joint profit-maximizing strategies, can be quashed by the imposition or threat of imposition of "the squeeze."

Another related argument attacks vertical integration as a barrier to entry. The threat of a squeeze is alleged to apply to potential entrants, thereby re-ducing the vigor of competition. In addition, the absolute capital requirements for entry into the industry are larger than entry into only one stage.

> Going firms are surely aware of the trouble they can make for poten-tial entrants through vertical integration, especially through their control of distributive outlets. Integrated gasoline refiners acquire or control many of the better street and highway locations for service sta-tions and lease them to operators at prices that probably yield profits on some of the leased facilities that are below the cost of borrowed capital. But the service station places the company's brand name be-fore the public and stimulates the sale of its gasoline. And the control of good locations complicates life for the entrant refiners who must either buy up his own station sites or deal with such "greasy-rag" inde-pendent sites as he can find.[29]

Carrying this argument even further, we find that even the character of competition can be changed.

> The integrated firm . . . has chosen to take on a heavier burden of fixed costs in order to gain lower average costs of production or greater cer-

tainty about his operation. He loses flexibility in the process . . . [and] therefore has a natural preference for stability in the market place.[30]

This latter argument loses credibility if competition is considered from a long-run perspective where all costs are variable.

The oligopoly price arguments seem rather irrelevant to an environment in which the primary argument centered on downstream losses and upstream profits. Presumably, the squeeze is only a temporary phenomenon whose long-term purpose is to raise prices and profits downstream. Since the FRS is being designed for long-term use, it should be responsive to detecting possible oligopolistic behavior. The changes in the market caused by OPEC and various regulations, as well as the removal of the oil depletion allowance, could well turn a topic of little concern today into a future policy issue. Indeed, one future trend could be a tendency toward more profitable marketing by the integrated companies, accomplished by rationalization of the marketing segment. Rationalization implies a greater number of high volume, company-operated gasoline stations and fewer independent branded dealers.[31]

It is instructive to compare vertical integration with its alternatives vis-à-vis the question of anticompetitive behavior.[32] The substitutes for ownership, where vertical control is desired, are all restrictive contractual arrangements, most of which are illegal per se under the antitrust laws. These contractual arrangements include franchises (territorial restrictions), exclusive dealerships, tied sales, resale price maintenance, and requirements contracts.[33] Given that the alternatives are illegal, it should not be surprising to find a bias toward more observed vertical integration. The decision in the Schwinn case, for example, creates a double standard for evaluating territorial restrictions on downstream sales.[34] Restrictions were found legal on consignment sales (where no title was taken by the wholesalers), but illegal (per se) on contract sales (where title was taken). An incentive to integrate was established, although a recent decision has overturned the precedent. The Schwinn decision was overturned by the Supreme Court in *Continental TV, Inc., et al. v. GTE Sylvania,* where the verical restrictions were found legal if their primary purpose was for good business reasons.

The question remains as to whether vertical integration undertaken for efficiency reasons can also enhance oligopolistic coordination and discourage entry. The likely answer is "yes." If any analysis of the net benefits is to be undertaken, it must look at both sides of the competitive trade-off. Recognition of the antitrust-induced bias toward integration and away from market contracting in situations where coordinated strategies are efficient should temper the enthusiasm of observers of a high degree of vertical integration.

Another argument against vertical integration concerns market foreclosure. This alleges that integration precludes independents from either sources of supply or, more commonly, outlets for sales, since the integrated company would not buy from the independent. The SBKM study found evidence of no particular foreclosure problems for refiners. Discussion of allegations of vertical monopolization need not concern us here, in that monopoly structure is absent from the industry. Even if industry profits were somehow jointly maximized, the literature on the topic assures us that no gains are likely from extending the monopoly to two or more stages in the vertical chain.[35]

One argument against vertical integration in petroleum concerns the loss of information when transactions take place internally in large segments of the industry. Clearly, there is asymmetry of information between integrated firms and independents. The lack of information available could act as a barrier to entry and an obstacle to good performance. What is paradoxical is that this dearth of information is itself a motivation for integration.[36] Improved information could enhance competition in the market place. Collection of data that purports to mirror these internal transactions may not result in improved information. In fact, conclusions drawn from these internal company transfers may cause possible industry entrants to make incorrect decisions regarding the desirability of entry.

## Summary

Understanding the reasons for vertical integration is beneficial at two stages. First, the understanding assists in designing regulatory systems by assuring that the design criteria consider the institutional features of the industry. Second, an understanding of the economics of vertical integration enables the policy maker to use data to address a complete range of policy issues—those that are important today and those that have yet to be identified, but will be important in the future.

The economic policy maker is aware that today's problems may be tomorrow's objectives. For example, while many of today's policy questions may concern industry profits, tomorrow's questions may concern the generation of sufficient profits to ensure resource development. Because of the fast pace of the changing energy environment, regulatory information systems should be designed to accommodate the characteristics of the industry and should not be designed to address specific and short-term problems. The latter is myopic and could result in a rigid, obsolete, and useless system.

Specifically, economic hypotheses about vertical integration are necessary to evaluate the potential usefulness of economic information in assessing various competitive hypotheses by analyzing transaction costs and scale economies. The data should afford the policy maker the opportunity to focus on the costs of market contracting and compare them to the costs of long-term contracts and the costs of internal organization, thereby enabling policies to be based on the relative efficiencies or inefficiencies of vertical integration. The data should also assist in the analysis of scale economies resulting from vertical integration and the implications economies of the scale have for competition, regulatory policy, and resource development. These are difficult questions and will not be easily answered. Refinery operating expenses, capacity, and capacity utilization data can be collected for major petroleum companies. However, these are accounting data, and not the economic data preferred for empirical testing. The strength of conclusions to be drawn from this analysis will necessarily be subject to the limitations of the data, as discussed in chapter 6.

Vertical integration should be considered when addressing risk and capital costs within the industry. The policy maker should determine if integration reduces business risk and, therefore, capital costs. Time series analysis of capital costs should assist with this question. Vertical integration should also be considered when addressing anticompetitive behavior. Specific concerns include whether vertical integration facilitates oligopolistic coordination, barriers to entry, and market foreclosure, issues discussed in the previous chapter.

**Notes**

1. *Standard Oil Company of New Jersey* v. *U.S.* 1, 47, 76 (1911).

2. Most notably, J.S. McGee, "Predatory Price Cutting: The Standard Oil (N.J.) Case," *Journal of Law and Economics,* October 1958, pp. 137-69.

3. A.M. Johnson, "Lessons of the Standard Oil Divestiture," in E.J. Mitchell (ed.), *Vertical Integration in the Oil Industry* (Washington, D.C., American Enterprise Institute, 1976).

4. *Ibid.,* p. 194.

5. M. Adelman, *The World Petroleum Market* (Baltimore, Johns Hopkins University Press, 1972), p. 99.

6. See M.G. DeChazeau and A.E. Kahn, *Integration and Competition in the Petroleum Industry* (New Haven, Conn., Yale University Press, 1959), for an early statement of these arguments.

7. R. Mancke, *The Failure of U.S. Energy Policy* (New York: Columbia University Press, 1974), chapter 7.

8. Transfer pricing is discussed in detail in chapters 4 and 5.

9. Adelman, *The World Petroleum Market,* p. 160.

10. *Ibid.,* p. 164.

11. O. Williamson, *Markets and Hierarchies: Analysis and Antitrust Implications* (New York: Free Press, 1975).

12. D. Teece, *Vertical Integration and Vertical Divestiture in the U.S. Petroleum Industry* (Stanford, Ca., Stanford University Press, 1976).

13. *Ibid.,* from abstract.

14. A. Marshall, *Principles of Economics* (London, Macmillan, 1961), book V, ninth (var.) ed., p. 366.

15. K. Arrow, "Limited Knowledge and Economic Analysis," *American Economic Review,* vol. 64, no. 1, March, 1974, pp. 1-20.

16. Most notably, Frank Hahn, Presidential Address to the Econometric Society, 1968.

17. Teece, *Vertical Integration,* chapter 3.

18. F.M. Scherer, A Beckenstein, E. Kaufer, and R.D. Murphy. *The Economics of Multi-Plant Operation: An International Comparisons Study* (Cambridge, Mass., Harvard University Press, 1975).

19. Since efficient capacity increments are large, relative to total company sales, the single-refinery company must either underutilize capacity (by investing ahead of demand) or buy someone else's refined product (when investment lags behind demand) much of the time. The multiplant operator can transship excess production from one regional market to another and, therefore, gains a strategic advantage. If swaps among refiners are readily available, these advantages are lost.

20. SBKM, *The Economics of Multi-Plant Operation,* p. 292.

21. *Ibid.,* p. 292.

22. *Ibid.,* pp. 257-58.

23. A. Beckenstein, "The Economics of Production and Distribution as They Impact Small Business," *Journal of Contemporary Business,* Spring 1976, pp. 25-45.

24. *Ibid.,* p. 43.

25. See J.G. McLean and R.W. Haigh, *The Growth of Integrated Oil Companies* (Boston Mass., Harvard Business School, 1954). See also L. Cookenboo, *Crude Oil Pipelines and Competition in the Oil Industry* (Cambridge, Mass., Harvard University Press, 1955) for more examples.

26. E.J. Mitchell, "Capital Cost Savings of Vertical Integration," in E.J. Mitchell (ed.), *Vertical Integration in the Oil Industry.* (Washington, D.C., American Enterprise Institute, 1976).

27. L.E. Grayson, *Economics of Energy* (Princeton, N.J., Darwin Press, 1975), pp. XI-XIII.

28. H.L. Gabel, *A Simultaneous Equation Analysis of Industrial Structure and Performance,* unpublished dissertation, University of Pennsylvania, 1977.

29. R.E. Caves, *American Industry: Structure, Conduct, Performance* (Englewood Cliffs, N.J., Prentice-Hall, Inc., 1977) 4th ed., p. 44.

30. *Ibid.,* p. 44.

31. See, for example, J. Tanner, "Texaco is Pruning Marketing Activities, Putting Emphasis on Profit, Not Volume," *Wall Street Journal,* March 16 and 17, 1978.

32. This discussion borrows ideas expressed in W.J. Liebeler, "Integration and Competition," in E.J. Mitchell (ed.), *Vertical Integration in the Oil Industry* (Washington, D.C., American Enterprise Institute, 1976).

33. See *Standard Oil Co. of California et al.* v. *U.S.* 337 U.S. 293 (1949) for a relevant case in petroleum.

34. *U.S.* v. *Arnold Schwinn and Co., et al.,* 388 U.S. 365 (1967).

35. The exchange of views among (1) Martin Perry, (2) John Haring and David Kaserman, and (3) Melvin Greenhut and H. Ohta, in the March 1978 *American Economic Review* reinforces this conclusion that is discussed clearly in W.J. Liebeler, "Integration and Competition," in E.J. Mitchell (ed.), *Vertical Integration in the Oil Industry* (Washington, D.C., American Enterprise Institute, 1976), p. 22-24. See also, F. Warren-Boulton, *Vertical Control of Markets,* (Cambridge, Ballinger Publishing, 1978).

36. See K.J. Arrow, "Vertical Integration and Communication," *Bell Journal of Economics,* Fall 1975, pp. 173-83.

**Part IV
The Problem Reduced:
Different Measures for
Different Uses**

# 8

## Sources of Market Price Information

The starting point for determining a transfer price based on a market price when actual third party transactions are not available is to identify sources of published prices. Any published price series will then need to be adjusted for special product characteristics, geographical differences, financing arrangements, or other elements that may affect the value of a transaction. The authors determined that three sources of published petroleum product prices had potential as the foundation for a market-based transfer price. They are:

*Platt's Oilgram Price Service* and
*Platt's Oil Handbook (Platt's)*
McGraw-Hill, Inc.

Petroleum Product Prices and Price Indexes
*Wholesale Price Index* (WPI)
Bureau of Labor Statistics
Department of Labor

*Monthly Petroleum Product Price Report* (FEA-P302)
Energy Information Administration
Department of Energy

For each source, the authors examined the following areas:

*Description of data base:*
Publisher of the data
Purpose of the publication
Other uses

*Description of data elements:*
Source of data
Products included
Regions included
Transaction pricing point
Basis of Price

*Ability to validate data*

*Specific problems with the data base*

This chapter includes the results of the data base study and compares actual data points from each source to illustrate the range of variation among the various data bases that purport to measure the same product.

### Platt's Oilgram Price Service and Oil Price Handbook (Platt's)

#### Description of Data Base

*Platt's Oilgram Price Service* is published each business day throughout the year by McGraw-Hill Publications. The *Oilgram Price Service,* as well as its companion paper, *Platt's Oilgram News Service,* provides subscribers with current news of interest to the international petroleum industry.

The *Oilgram News Service* touches such wideranging issues as free world crude petroleum production, federal government reports regarding natural gas supplies, and political issues that may affect petroleum interests. The *Oilgram Price Service* focuses on price issues and includes news articles of interest to its readers as well as price surveys for sales of products at selected locations. The *Oilgram Price Service* rotates the publication of surveys so that not all products and markets are listed each day. The price survey is the portion of the *Oilgram Price Service* of interest to us here.

McGraw-Hill also publishes *Platt's Oil Price Handbook* at the end of each calendar year. The prices published in the handbook include compilations of the daily price surveys as well as price reports from other sources. All three publications serve subscribers who are members of the oil industry, industry analysts, and others interested in current trends of the petroleum and related markets.

In addition to monitoring the trends in the petroleum market, subscribers use *Platt's Oilgram Price Service* as a reference point for internal pricing policies and planning activities. For example, Company G, referenced earlier, uses the estimated Gulf Coast cargo spot gasoline prices published by the Price Service as the starting point for determining its internal gasoline transfer price from the refining unit to the marketing unit. Prior to price controls, Companies B and F used gasoline prices quoted by Platt's as the basis for their gasoline transfer prices. These two companies believe that federal price controls destroy the utility of Platt's prices and as a result no longer use them for transfer prices.

#### Description of Data Elements

*Platt's Oilgram Price Service* collects its data elements through telephone surveys of selected integrated oil companies that are active in the market. The prices, rounded to the nearest hundredth of a cent, are checked periodically. Individuals at Platt's call oil company supply departments when there is an indication that

the price of a product may change. Prices are confirmed with oil company suppliers and sometimes verified by other industry sources. Daily published prices
for products show the price ranges for each product at a particular transaction
point. For example, on March 10, 1978, Platt's reported that premium gasoline
had sold for between $.3965 and $.409 a gallon on March 9 from terminals
located at the New York harbor.

On an annual basis, *Platt's Oil Price Handbook* translates the daily price
surveys into average monthly price ranges for products in a variety of markets.
In the 1976 *Handbook,* Platt's reported the monthly average wholesale price of
gasoline in twenty-seven U.S. cities.

The basis for the prices published in the *Oilgram Price Service* and the *Oil
Price Handbook* varies with each product. They are either "sales prices, or quota-
tions, or general offers, or posted prices."[1] A spokesman for Platt's indicated
that the Gulf Coast cargo prices for gasoline, for example, are the weighted
average of actual sales for at least 20,000 barrels from large cargo ships in the
Gulf Coast ports.

In addition to wholesale gasoline prices, Platt's monitors the mid-month
prices of dealer tank wagon sales in fifty-five U.S. cities that are considered to be
representative of the total American gasoline market. A dealer tank wagon sale,
as defined by Platt's, is a sale by an integrated oil company to a gasoline retail
station dealer who sells the integrated oil company's brand.

For all prices surveyed by Platt's the transaction pricing point is FOB (free
on board) the refinery, pipeline, or tanker terminal. Normally, no transaction
point is specified when the prices are published. For example, March 9, 1978
price ranges were published for eighteen locations (districts) for five products
under the price series entitled "South and East Terminals." The type of terminal
at which the transaction took place varies with location, so that the reader may
be comparing sales from pipeline terminals in one location with sales made from
inland waterway barge terminals at another location. The explanatory notes in
the 1976 *Oil Price Handbook* indicate that prices not included in Platt's price
survey are:

> prices arrived at by discounts off a specified price; Market-date-of-
> shipment prices; prices named in contracts and prices arrived at in
> accordance with arrangements made prior to date of sale. Prices made
> to *brokers* and prices in inter-refinery transactions also are not con-
> sidered in the tables.[2] [emphasis added]

*Ability to Validate Data*

Neither the DOE nor McGraw-Hill has the ability to validate the data published
in *Platt's Oilgram Price Service* or *Platt's Oil Price Handbook.* The published

prices are received voluntarily. Companies determine which prices they will report and when they are reported.

### Specific Problems with the Data Base

In addition to the inability to validate data, there are several other problems with using Platt's as the main data base for a market transfer price. Individual transaction volumes and total volumes represented in the published prices are unknown. In many cases, the published prices are posted rather than actual prices. If the actual transaction volumes are small, the prices may not be representative of marketplace price trends. The transaction points vary and may include transportation differentials.

The prices are also influenced by the price survey methodology of calling selected suppliers and buyers for transactions information. The suppliers may choose to report higher priced sales, whereas the buyers may choose to report lower priced purchases. The prices are most useful when viewed as possible price ranges to be used as indicators of trends in a general geographical area.

In spite of these problems, oil companies throughout the industry look to *Platt's Oilgram Price Service* to check internal pricing policies because it is the only daily report available.

### Petroleum Product Prices and Price Indexes—Bureau of Labor Statistics

### Description of Data Base

The Bureau of Labor Statistics (BLS) of the Department of Labor publishes a monthly index of wholesale prices. One of the components of the *Wholesale Price Index* (*WPI*) is a set of indexes based on specified petroleum products (see table 8-1). Data collected in the BLS data base reflect price trends of the products. The price trends, as well as other trends in the *WPI*, are used by the federal government to measure changes in the general price level of the American economy.

The *WPI* is used extensively throughout industry and government agencies in budget development and review. In recent years, corporations have used the *WPI* to appraise inventories for the establishment of replacement costs for accounting records.

### Description of Data Elements

The current system used by the BLS began in July 1975. Each month forty-six petroleum companies respond on a voluntary and confidential basis to a mail questionnaire in which they state total sales revenues (dollars) and total sales volume (gallons) for several classes of customers purchasing eight product groups. The index is derived by dividing the total sales revenues by total sales volumes to arrive at a price per gallon. The BLS requests that companies exclude certain transactions, such as interplant and intracompany transfers and military sales.

Most of the wholesale prices used to make up the *WPI* are based on typical sales throughout the month. "Typical" sales are defined as those taking place on the Tuesday of the week containing the thirteenth day. For petroleum products, sales throughout the month are reported and, therefore, data published in the August index reflect prices for the month of July. Analysis conducted on the *WPI* should take that time lag into consideration.

The BLS examines prices within a geographical region for classes of customers purchasing each product. The regions are made up of a set of complete states. For example, the index for the West South Central region consists of sales to resellers in Arkansas, Louisiana, Oklahoma, and Texas. Although regions remain constant for all products, the classes of customers change depending on the method of distribution for the product.

Data are collected for all three grades of gasoline: regular, premium, and unleaded. Sample reports included here were published prior to the inclusion of unleaded gasoline. For each grade, prices in each of the nine regions are determined by three types of sales: dealer tank wagons to retail outlets, jobbers, and commercial consumers.

General guidelines provide some direction to the company representative completing the form, but a great deal of interpretation is still required to fit sales for a range of products into the limited categories mentioned earlier. For example, the transaction pricing point is defined by the BLS as the "first significant commercial transaction (in the distribution chain) in the United States." The company representatives use their own discretion, within the basic BLS guidelines, to determine which sales should be included.

*Ability to Validate Data*

All reports submitted to the BLS are voluntary and confidential. No audits are authorized, but BLS personnel call the oil companies when they have questions regarding a company's submission of data. For example, companies are asked to verify prices that change by more than 10 percent in any one month. Recently, BLS personnel have been checking with oil companies to determine if intracompany transfers are included in the sales volumes and revenues. The conclusion is that in some cases oil companies do include transfers of gasoline to company owned and operated retail stations in reported sales volumes and revenues for dealer tank wagons. The method of determining the value assigned to the transfers varies by company.

**Table 8–1**
**Wholesale Prices and Price Indexes—1976**

| Code No. | Commodity | Other Index Bases | Annual Average | Jan. | Feb. |
|---|---|---|---|---|---|
| 0571 | *Gasoline* | 1967 | 254.0 | 247.7 | 246.6 |
| 02 | Regular | Feb/73 | 233.6 | 227.3 | 226.4 |
| 0201 | Dealer tank-wagon to retail outlets | Feb/73 | 218.1 | 213.0 | 212.1 |
| 01 | New England | | 107.1 | 105.2 | 104.7 |
| 02 | Middle Atlantic | | 107.1 | 105.5 | 105.9 |
| 03 | South Atlantic | | 107.3 | 105.4 | 104.2 |
| 04 | East North Central | | 108.4 | 105.6 | 105.1 |
| 05 | West South Central | | 108.8 | 105.8 | 104.9 |
| 06 | East South Central | | 107.6 | 105.2 | 104.4 |
| 07 | West North Central | | 110.5 | 107.1 | 106.6 |
| 08 | Mountain | | 112.4 | 108.8 | 109.1 |
| 09 | Pacific | | 108.7 | 105.7 | 106.1 |
| 0202 | Sales to jobbers | Feb/73 | 256.4 | 247.9 | 246.7 |
| 01 | New England | | 108.6 | 105.8 | 105.3 |
| 02 | Middle Atlantic | | 108.3 | 106.0 | 105.0 |
| 03 | South Atlantic | | 108.1 | 015.6 | 104.7 |
| 04 | East North Central | | 109.2 | 104.9 | 104.9 |
| 05 | West South Central | | 108.7 | 104.7 | 104.1 |
| 06 | East South Central | | 108.5 | 105.4 | 104.4 |
| 07 | West North Central | | 109.5 | 105.5 | 104.7 |
| 08 | Mountain | | 107.2 | 103.2 | 104.3 |
| 09 | Pacific | | 107.6 | 104.5 | 104.6 |
| 0203 | Commercial consumers | Feb/73 | 248.5 | 242.7 | 242.1 |
| 01 | New England | | 107.9 | 105.4 | 104.9 |
| 02 | Middle Atlantic | | 107.8 | 105.0 | 105.1 |
| 03 | South Atlantic | | 108.5 | 106.5 | 106.3 |
| 04 | East North Central | | 106.7 | 104.8 | 104.2 |
| 05 | West South Central | | 107.5 | 102.6 | 102.6 |
| 06 | East South Central | | 107.1 | 104.4 | 103.4 |
| 07 | West North Central | | 108.1 | 106.4 | 106.1 |
| 08 | Mountain | | 108.3 | 106.0 | 106.0 |
| 09 | Pacific | | 107.2 | 105.4 | 105.7 |
| 03 | Premium | Feb/73 | 207.2 | 203.0 | 201.9 |
| 0301 | Dealer tank-wagon to retail outlets | Feb/73 | 198.1 | 194.9 | 193.6 |
| 01 | New England | | 106.9 | 105.7 | 104.8 |
| 02 | Middle Atlantic | | 107.0 | 105.8 | 104.9 |
| 03 | South Atlantic | | 106.9 | 105.2 | 104.6 |
| 04 | East North Central | | 107.3 | 105.0 | 104.7 |
| 05 | West South Central | | 108.4 | 106.1 | 105.0 |
| 06 | East South Central | | 106.8 | 104.8 | 104.1 |
| 07 | West North Central | | 108.8 | 106.2 | 105.7 |
| 08 | Mountain | | 107.0 | 104.6 | 104.6 |
| 09 | Pacific | | 107.1 | 105.3 | 104.8 |
| 0302 | Sales to jobbers | Feb/73 | 227.8 | 221.5 | 220.6 |
| 01 | New England | | 108.4 | 105.7 | 106.1 |
| 02 | Middle Atlantic | | 108.6 | 106.0 | 105.2 |

| Mar. | Apr. | May | June | July | Aug. | Sept. | Oct. | Nov. | Dec. |
|------|------|-----|------|------|------|-------|------|------|------|
| 241.4 | 238.6 | 240.1 | 249.0 | 259.8 | 264.0 | 266.1 | 265.8 | 264.9 | 263.4 |
| 221.7 | 219.1 | 220.6 | 229.2 | 239.4 | 243.2 | 245.0 | 244.7 | 243.8 | 242.2 |
|  |  |  |  |  |  |  |  |  |  |
| 207.3 | 205.1 | 206.2 | 213.8 | 222.6 | 226.5 | 228.5 | 228.3 | 227.5 | 225.8 |
| 102.0 | 100.9 | 101.5 | 105.1 | 109.5 | 112.0 | 112.2 | 111.7 | 111.0 | 109.8 |
| 102.3 | 100.8 | 101.3 | 104.7 | 109.1 | 110.8 | 112.2 | 111.8 | 111.2 | 109.9 |
| 102.6 | 101.4 | 101.7 | 105.2 | 109.5 | 111.2 | 112.5 | 112.0 | 111.4 | 110.3 |
| 103.3 | 101.8 | 102.5 | 106.5 | 110.5 | 112.8 | 113.4 | 113.2 | 113.3 | 112.7 |
| 102.7 | 102.5 | 103.1 | 107.2 | 111.5 | 113.6 | 114.6 | 114.1 | 113.2 | 112.3 |
| 102.3 | 101.5 | 101.9 | 106.0 | 110.3 | 111.8 | 112.7 | 112.3 | 111.9 | 111.1 |
| 105.1 | 103.6 | 104.3 | 108.5 | 112.9 | 114.6 | 115.6 | 116.0 | 116.1 | 115.5 |
| 106.6 | 105.9 | 106.0 | 109.3 | 114.0 | 116.3 | 118.0 | 119.4 | 117.9 | 117.5 |
| 102.4 | 101.8 | 102.5 | 105.7 | 110.7 | 112.5 | 113.8 | 114.5 | 114.3 | 114.3 |
|  |  |  |  |  |  |  |  |  |  |
| 242.4 | 239.6 | 241.8 | 252.1 | 263.9 | 268.1 | 269.5 | 269.1 | 268.4 | 267.1 |
| 102.8 | 102.0 | 102.5 | 106.4 | 111.1 | 113.3 | 115.2 | 114.2 | 113.0 | 111.6 |
| 101.9 | 101.1 | 101.6 | 106.1 | 111.4 | 113.6 | 114.7 | 113.9 | 112.8 | 111.7 |
| 102.3 | 101.3 | 101.6 | 105.8 | 110.9 | 112.9 | 114.1 | 113.5 | 112.3 | 111.8 |
| 103.1 | 102.0 | 103.2 | 107.6 | 112.4 | 114.2 | 114.7 | 114.9 | 114.6 | 113.9 |
| 102.3 | 101.1 | 102.6 | 107.8 | 112.9 | 113.9 | 114.4 | 114.1 | 113.6 | 113.1 |
| 102.9 | 101.8 | 102.1 | 106.4 | 111.4 | 113.3 | 114.4 | 114.0 | 113.5 | 112.8 |
| 103.7 | 101.8 | 103.5 | 108.1 | 112.9 | 114.6 | 114.0 | 114.9 | 115.3 | 114.6 |
| 101.7 | 100.2 | 100.9 | 104.7 | 109.5 | 111.2 | 112.0 | 113.0 | 113.0 | 112.5 |
| 102.4 | 101.2 | 102.4 | 104.3 | 109.1 | 111.0 | 112.0 | 111.7 | 113.6 | 114.5 |
|  |  |  |  |  |  |  |  |  |  |
| 237.0 | 233.3 | 235.0 | 243.5 | 255.6 | 258.3 | 260.2 | 260.0 | 258.2 | 256.4 |
| 102.5 | 101.2 | 102.2 | 106.0 | 110.4 | 111.9 | 113.1 | 113.0 | 112.6 | 111.5 |
| 102.1 | 101.7 | 102.6 | 106.8 | 111.3 | 112.7 | 113.4 | 112.1 | 111.1 | 110.0 |
| 103.5 | 102.1 | 102.4 | 106.9 | 111.9 | 112.7 | 113.4 | 112.9 | 111.9 | 111.3 |
| 102.3 | 100.2 | 101.0 | 104.5 | 109.3 | 110.5 | 111.1 | 111.2 | 110.6 | 110.1 |
| 101.2 | 100.6 | 101.9 | 107.4 | 114.9 | 113.0 | 112.9 | 112.0 | 110.6 | 110.2 |
| 101.5 | 100.9 | 101.8 | 106.1 | 110.6 | 111.6 | 112.0 | 111.5 | 111.1 | 110.3 |
| 104.0 | 102.1 | 102.7 | 105.8 | 110.0 | 111.7 | 113.1 | 112.8 | 112.2 | 110.0 |
| 103.5 | 102.9 | 102.2 | 104.6 | 109.5 | 111.4 | 113.3 | 114.1 | 113.5 | 112.1 |
| 102.3 | 100.1 | 100.4 | 103.0 | 108.6 | 111.3 | 112.5 | 113.3 | 112.1 | 112.1 |
|  |  |  |  |  |  |  |  |  |  |
| 197.6 | 195.5 | 196.1 | 202.8 | 211.2 | 214.5 | 216.5 | 216.4 | 215.9 | 214.8 |
|  |  |  |  |  |  |  |  |  |  |
| 189.2 | 187.1 | 187.8 | 193.8 | 201.5 | 204.7 | 206.9 | 206.9 | 206.4 | 204.9 |
| 101.8 | 100.1 | 100.7 | 104.9 | 109.6 | 111.1 | 112.1 | 111.6 | 110.6 | 110.0 |
| 102.1 | 100.7 | 101.1 | 104.8 | 109.1 | 110.7 | 112.2 | 111.7 | 111.1 | 110.0 |
| 102.6 | 101.3 | 101.4 | 104.7 | 108.7 | 110.3 | 111.7 | 111.3 | 110.8 | 109.7 |
| 102.8 | 101.3 | 101.7 | 105.1 | 109.1 | 110.9 | 111.8 | 112.0 | 111.9 | 111.2 |
| 102.9 | 102.4 | 103.0 | 106.6 | 110.6 | 112.5 | 113.6 | 113.1 | 112.8 | 111.8 |
| 102.0 | 101.4 | 101.4 | 104.9 | 108.9 | 110.2 | 111.3 | 111.0 | 111.0 | 110.2 |
| 104.0 | 102.5 | 103.1 | 106.7 | 110.8 | 112.1 | 113.3 | 113.6 | 114.0 | 113.2 |
| 102.0 | 101.4 | 101.4 | 104.0 | 108.2 | 110.3 | 111.5 | 112.5 | 111.7 | 111.4 |
| 102.0 | 101.1 | 101.5 | 104.0 | 108.4 | 110.2 | 111.4 | 112.2 | 112.1 | 111.7 |
|  |  |  |  |  |  |  |  |  |  |
| 216.5 | 214.5 | 215.0 | 223.4 | 233.4 | 236.9 | 238.6 | 238.2 | 237.8 | 237.1 |
| 103.4 | 102.6 | 102.8 | 106.4 | 110.7 | 112.7 | 114.3 | 113.2 | 112.1 | 110.8 |
| 102.7 | 103.2 | 101.9 | 107.9 | 111.4 | 113.1 | 114.2 | 113.4 | 112.3 | 111.4 |

*Table 8-1 continued*

| Code No. | | Commodity | Other Index Bases | Annual Average | Jan. | Feb. |
|---|---|---|---|---|---|---|
| | 03 | South Atlantic | | 107.3 | 105.1 | 104.4 |
| | 04 | East North Central | | 109.2 | 106.8 | 106.0 |
| | 05 | West South Central | | 107.3 | 104.5 | 103.4 |
| | 06 | East South Central | | 107.7 | 105.0 | 104.0 |
| | 07 | West North Central | | 105.0 | 102.1 | 101.2 |
| | 08 | Mountain | | 108.1 | 104.8 | 104.4 |
| | 09 | Pacific | | 107.8 | 102.7 | 104.4 |
| 0303 | | Commercial consumers | Feb/73 | 232.2 | 226.9 | 226.4 |
| | 01 | New England | | 109.5 | 108.3 | 104.8 |
| | 02 | Middle Atlantic | | 108.5 | 104.8 | 105.2 |
| | 03 | South Atlantic | | 107.4 | 105.6 | 105.2 |
| | 04 | East North Central | | 105.2 | 103.4 | 103.1 |
| | 05 | West South Central | | 105.8 | 102.1 | 102.0 |
| | 06 | East South Central | | 108.1 | 105.0 | 105.3 |
| | 07 | West North Central | | 105.6 | 99.4 | 102.9 |
| | 08 | Mountain | | 106.9 | 102.7 | 105.9 |
| | 09 | Pacific | | 103.6 | 104.6 | 104.1 |
| 0572 | | Light distillate | 1967 | 312.3 | 210.5 | 316.6 |
| | 0201 | Kerosene to resellers | Feb/73 | 256.3 | 256.3 | 256.8 |
| | 01 | New England | | 105.9 | 106.4 | 106.5 |
| | 02 | Middle Atlantic | | 107.6 | 108.4 | 108.7 |
| | 03 | South Atlantic | | 108.9 | 108.3 | 109.0 |
| | 04 | East North Central | | 111.2 | 112.0 | 111.6 |

Source: *Wholesale Prices and Price Indexes Supplement,* 1977. Data for 1976 U.S. Department of Labor, Bureau of Labor Statistics.

## Specific Problems with Data

Although the BLS performs analytical tests on collected data, it does not have the authority to audit the companies directly. The sample of prices is larger than that collected by *Platt's,* but represents forty-six companies that range from large integrated companies to smaller, more localized companies. Some prices may include adjustments for credit terms, quantity discounts, or franchise services.

In addition to the inability to audit data, the instructions are sufficiently vague and the product categories inclusive enough that many decisions regarding how to report data remain with the individual company reporters. The recent discovery that intracompany transfers are included in some of the reported sales volumes and revenues represents one problem that resulted from the lack of definitive guidelines. Although companies are cooperative with the BLS, the data base is too uneven for DOE purposes because of the discretionary decisions that reporters must make.

| Mar. | Apr. | May | June | July | Aug. | Sept. | Oct. | Nov. | Dec. |
|------|------|------|------|------|------|------|------|------|------|
| 102.6 | 101.2 | 100.7 | 104.8 | 109.5 | 111.4 | 112.6 | 112.3 | 111.6 | 111.0 |
| 104.2 | 102.6 | 103.4 | 106.7 | 111.4 | 113.2 | 113.8 | 114.2 | 113.9 | 113.8 |
| 101.2 | 100.2 | 101.3 | 105.8 | 110.9 | 112.4 | 112.6 | 112.1 | 111.3 | 111.6 |
| 103.0 | 101.7 | 101.6 | 105.2 | 110.0 | 111.8 | 113.0 | 112.7 | 112.3 | 111.8 |
| 100.2 | 98.2 | 99.8 | 103.6 | 108.1 | 109.1 | 108.7 | 109.5 | 110.0 | 109.7 |
| 102.3 | 101.1 | 102.3 | 106.2 | 110.7 | 112.1 | 112.7 | 113.3 | 113.5 | 113.7 |
| 101.8 | 100.9 | 103.0 | 105.0 | 110.1 | 111.9 | 113.1 | 112.5 | 114.2 | 114.3 |
| 222.6 | 218.3 | 219.8 | 227.2 | 235.9 | 240.7 | 242.7 | 242.4 | 241.7 | 242.3 |
| 104.3 | 101.9 | 101.9 | 107.8 | 113.0 | 113.9 | 115.2 | 114.6 | 115.1 | 113.3 |
| 103.0 | 102.3 | 103.3 | 107.3 | 112.9 | 114.1 | 114.4 | 113.3 | 110.7 | 110.9 |
| 102.8 | 101.3 | 101.9 | 105.7 | 110.2 | 111.4 | 111.6 | 111.7 | 110.8 | 110.4 |
| 102.0 | 100.5 | 99.3 | 101.1 | 105.8 | 107.4 | 109.3 | 110.0 | 110.1 | 110.8 |
| 100.2 | 98.5 | 100.7 | 106.4 | 109.7 | 111.7 | 110.9 | 109.0 | 108.2 | 110.2 |
| 102.9 | 101.9 | 102.8 | 107.5 | 111.9 | 111.6 | 112.8 | 112.5 | 111.8 | 111.0 |
| 101.0 | 99.3 | 100.9 | 107.1 | 106.5 | 112.0 | 108.4 | 112.1 | 108.4 | 109.0 |
| 102.2 | 102.2 | 101.1 | 102.3 | 108.3 | 110.4 | 110.4 | 112.3 | 110.5 | 114.3 |
| 102.0 | 97.4 | 97.9 | 99.0 | 101.3 | 105.2 | 107.4 | 107.5 | 108.4 | 108.5 |
| 313.9 | 311.2 | 306.7 | 303.8 | 305.4 | 309.2 | 311.5 | 316.0 | 320.2 | 323.2 |
| 255.0 | 252.2 | 249.7 | 250.7 | 253.4 | 255.7 | 257.9 | 259.6 | 261.8 | 266.1 |
| 106.5 | 104.3 | 104.3 | 104.3 | 104.0 | 104.9 | 105.7 | 106.4 | 107.5 | 109.9 |
| 107.2 | 106.0 | 104.4 | 104.2 | 106.3 | 106.5 | 108.7 | 109.0 | 110.0 | 111.9 |
| 108.3 | 107.3 | 106.6 | 106.9 | 107.4 | 108.9 | 109.5 | 110.2 | 110.9 | 113.6 |
| 110.9 | 109.6 | 108.1 | 109.5 | 111.1 | 110.6 | 111.4 | 112.2 | 113.8 | 114.0 |

## Monthly Petroleum Product Price Report—Form FEA-P302

*Description of Data Base*

In accordance with the Mandatory Petroleum Price Regulation and Section 13 of the Federal Energy Administration Act of 1974, the DOE publishes the *Monthly Petroleum Product Price Report.* The purpose of the report is to provide the data necessary for the DOE to execute its role in monitoring petroleum product prices,[3] and to facilitate the timely analysis of price and volume of sales data at the refined product level upon which the DOE will rely in determining conformity with the established petroleum policies.[4]

Data are submitted for all refiners who refine any of the more than twenty-five products included in the FEA-P302 requirements. After the filing, which is mandatory, the data for all companies are combined and published in the monthly report on an aggregated basis. As a public document, the monthly *Petroleum Product Price Report* is available for review by industry analysts and the general public (table 8-2).

**Table 8-2**
**Petroleum Product Price Report—June 1977**
*(cents per gallon)*

|  | 1975[a] | | | | | | 1976 | | | | | |
|---|---|---|---|---|---|---|---|---|---|---|---|---|
|  | *July* | *Aug.* | *Sept.* | *Oct.* | *Nov.* | *Dec.* | *Jan.* | *Feb.* | *Mar.* | *Apr.* | *May* | *June* |
| *Motor gasoline* | | | | | | | | | | | | |
| Premium–wholesale | 36.8 | 37.6 | 37.6 | 37.5 | 36.8 | 36.2 | 36.1 | 35.3 | 34.8 | 35.2 | 36.6 | 38.3 |
| Premium–DTW | 41.1 | 41.8 | 42.1 | 41.6 | 41.3 | 41.1 | 40.9 | 40.7 | 39.4 | 39.6 | 40.8 | 42.2 |
| Premium–retail | 46.0 | 48.5 | 47.9 | 47.5 | 46.8 | 46.4 | 46.0 | 45.9 | 44.9 | 45.1 | 46.5 | 48.3 |
| Regular–wholesale | 34.5 | 35.3 | 35.4 | 34.9 | 34.2 | 33.8 | 33.4 | 32.8 | 32.4 | 32.8 | 34.3 | 36.0 |
| Regular–DTW | 37.7 | 38.5 | 38.8 | 38.5 | 37.9 | 37.7 | 37.5 | 36.6 | 36.2 | 36.3 | 37.6 | 39.2 |
| Regular–retail | 44.8 | 44.8 | 44.3 | 43.5 | 42.7 | 42.2 | 41.8 | 41.7 | 40.8 | 41.1 | 42.4 | 44.0 |
| No lead–wholesale | 35.6 | 36.1 | 36.3 | 35.9 | 35.5 | 35.2 | 34.9 | 34.3 | 33.7 | 34.0 | 35.3 | 37.0 |
| No lead–DTW | 39.1 | 39.7 | 39.9 | 39.7 | 39.3 | 39.1 | 38.9 | 38.1 | 37.5 | 37.6 | 38.8 | 40.3 |
| No lead–retail | 46.0 | 46.4 | 46.0 | 45.5 | 44.6 | 44.2 | 43.7 | 43.8 | 42.7 | 43.0 | 44.3 | 45.8 |
| Average | 37.4 | 38.1 | 38.3 | 37.8 | 37.3 | 37.0 | 36.7 | 36.1 | 35.5 | 35.7 | 37.2 | 38.7 |

|  | 1976 | | | | | | 1977 | | | | | |
|---|---|---|---|---|---|---|---|---|---|---|---|---|
|  | *July* | *Aug.* | *Sept.* | *Oct.* | *Nov.* | *Dec.* | *Jan.* | *Feb.* | *Mar.* | *Apr.* | *May*[b] | *June* |
| *Motor gasoline* | | | | | | | | | | | | |
| Premium–wholesale | 38.6 | 39.0 | 38.8 | 38.7 | 38.6 | 38.3 | 38.5 | 39.2 | 40.0 | 40.9 | 41.6 | 42.0 |
| Premium–DTW | 43.2 | 43.7 | 43.8 | 43.4 | 43.3 | 43.1 | 43.2 | 44.0 | 44.8 | 45.5 | 46.3 | 46.7 |
| Premium–retail | 48.6 | 48.6 | 48.4 | 48.2 | 48.1 | 47.0 | 47.0 | 47.6 | 48.4 | 49.3 | 50.1 | 50.7 |
| Regular–wholesale | 36.3 | 36.4 | 36.5 | 36.4 | 36.1 | 35.8 | 35.8 | 36.6 | 37.3 | 38.1 | 38.7 | 39.1 |
| Regular–DTW | 39.8 | 40.2 | 40.2 | 40.1 | 39.7 | 39.4 | 39.6 | 40.3 | 40.9 | 41.6 | 42.4 | 42.7 |
| Regular–retail | 43.9 | 44.0 | 43.8 | 43.6 | 43.4 | 42.8 | 42.3 | 42.9 | 43.5 | 44.6 | 45.2 | 45.8 |
| No lead–wholesale | 37.6 | 37.7 | 37.8 | 37.6 | 37.4 | 37.1 | 37.2 | 38.5 | 39.5 | 40.2 | 40.8 | 41.5 |
| No lead–DTW | 41.1 | 41.6 | 41.6 | 41.5 | 41.2 | 40.9 | 41.1 | 42.4 | 43.1 | 43.8 | 44.6 | 45.0 |
| No lead–retail | 46.4 | 46.4 | 46.0 | 46.0 | 45.7 | 45.2 | 45.1 | 46.2 | 46.9 | 47.9 | 48.8 | 49.4 |
| Average | 39.3 | 39.4 | 39.5 | 39.3 | 39.1 | 38.8 | 38.9 | 39.7 | 40.4 | 41.2 | R41.8 | 42.3 |

Source: FEA.

R = Revised data.

[a]Data are not available prior to July 1975.

[b]Preliminary data.

*Description of Data Elements*

Data are collected on the mandatory monthly questionnaire FEA-P302 which requests total sales revenue and total volumes for different levels of distribution within various product categories. For example, the FEA-P302 collects revenue and volume information about wholesale, retail, and dealer tank wagon sales of premium, regular, and no-lead gasoline. Prices published in the monthly report are the sum of all refiners' sales revenues divided by the sum of all refiners' sales volumes. The prices are published to the nearest one-tenth of a cent per gallon.

No specific transaction pricing point is stated in the instructions for completing the form. The company personnel completing the form must decide whether the sales should be recorded as wholesale, dealer tank wagon, or retail. Sales considered to be wholesale may be made at the refinery gate or the product terminal. The definition of sale is "the passing of title from the seller to the buyer for a price."[5] Therefore, intracompany transfers should not be included.

*Ability to Validate Data*

The DOE is authorized to audit companies that submit data on the FEA-P302. Audits are conducted only if data appear to be outside the expected ranges. The unaudited data are aggregated and published on receipt.

**Reliability of Independent Data Bases**

In the previous section, three separate data bases were discussed: *Platt's Oilgram Price Service, WPI,* and the DOEs FEA-P302. These data bases are summarized in table 8-3.

Prices for gasoline were examined to determine the variability among sources of data. The prices have been plotted for the period July 1975 through December 1976, to determine how sensitive they are to different product definitions and collection techniques. These are presented graphically in figures 8-1 and 8-2.

*Regular Gasoline Prices*

The prices of regular gasoline to two sets of customers, dealer tank wagons and jobbers, are represented by a graph in figure 8-1. Dealer tank wagon prices from the three independent data sources cluster together at a level 2 to 4 cents per gallon higher than prices to jobbers. During the eighteen months studied, the dealer tank wagon price differential among *Platt's Oil Price Handbook,* FEA-P302 and *WPI* national average never exceeded 1 cent. The dealer tank wagon

**Table 8-3**
**Relevant Published Price Series**

| | Platt's Oilgram Price Service (Platt's) | Wholesale Price Index (WPI) | Monthly Petroleum Product Price Report FEA-P302 |
|---|---|---|---|
| Publisher of data | McGraw-Hill | Department of Labor, Bureau of Labor Statistics | Department of Energy, Energy Information Agency |
| Publication frequency | Daily, Monday through Friday, except for selected holidays. | Monthly | Monthly |
| Purpose of data | Apprise subscribers of current trends in petroleum and related markets. | Reflect price trends for petroleum products as part of the WPI. Allows federal government to measure changes in general price level. | Monitor petroleum product prices to determine conformity with established government petroleum policies. |
| Other uses | Reference point for oil companies developing internal and external pricing policies. | Budget making and review by government and private industry; appraising inventories to establish replacement costs. | Public document for outside analysis. |
| Source of data | Telephone surveys to selected oil companies. Specific transactions and posted prices. Not checked daily. | Forty-six petroleum companies respond to voluntary, confidential mail questionnaire. Price = total sales revenues ÷ total volumes. | Mandatory monthly questionnaire filed by all refiners of certain products. Price = sales revenues ÷ total volumes. |
| Products included | Three grades of motor gasoline, liquefied petroleum gas, distillates, fuel oils, lubes. | Three grades of motor gasoline, kerosene, commercial jet fuel, fuel oil #2, diesel to commercial users, residual fuels, several customer categories. | Three grades of motor gasoline, 4 grades of distillates, 5 grades of residual fuel, 3 grades of aviation fuel, kerosene and petrochemical feedstocks, and others. |
| Regions included | Regional coverage on some products. Regions not clearly defined. | Regional data available on all products. Regions equal defined group of states. | One national weighted average. |
| Transaction pricing point | FOB, refinery, pipeline terminal, or tanker terminal. | FOB production point. | Not defined. Sales are from refiners to third party as designated by particular product and level of sale. |
| Ability to validate data | None | Data submission is voluntary; not audited. | Individual companies can be audited. |
| Specific problems with data | Will not reveal sources, quantities traded, or number of prices. Prices often posted, not actual. | Submission is voluntary; not auditable. Companies determine sales and customer categories. | Only one national weighted average price is currently available. No detail data by type of customer or point of sale. Six-month delay in publication after data collection. |

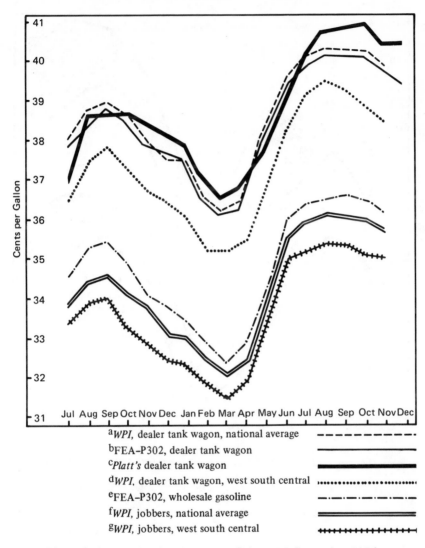

[a]*WPI*, dealer tank wagon, national average

[b]FEA–P302, dealer tank wagon

[c]*Platt's* dealer tank wagon

[d]*WPI*, dealer tank wagon, west south central

[e]FEA–P302, wholesale gasoline

[f]*WPI*, jobbers, national average

[g]*WPI*, jobbers, west south central

**Figure 8-1.** Regular Gasoline Prices July 1975–December 1976

price reported for the West South Central region to the *WPI* was consistently lower by approximately five-tenths of a cent.

The cluster of prices is significant for several reasons. First, the sales volumes reported to the three price series vary in size. The *WPI* volumes include all dealer tank wagon sales made by forty-six selected companies, whereas FEA-P302 volumes are for dealer tank wagon sales made by all refiners during the specified

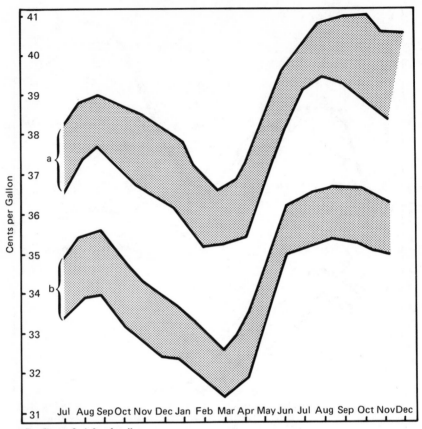

See figure 8-1 for detail.
[a]Outer bounds of gasoline dealer tank wagon prices from *WPI*, FEA-P302, and *Platt's*.
[b]Outer bounds of gasoline jobber and wholesale prices from *WPI* and FEA-P302.

**Figure 8-2.** Range of Gasoline Prices July 1975-December 1976

month. In spite of these volume differences, the average prices from the three price series track very closely.

Second, *Platt's Oil Price Handbook* prices are U.S. midmonthly prices averaged from fifty-five representative cities. Both FEA-P302 and *WPI* represent monthly national weighted average prices.

Prices for regular gasoline sales to jobbers are also clustered, although not as closely as sales for dealer tank wagons. As shown in figure 8-1, the prices reported to DOE on the FEA-P302 are consistently two-tenths to eight-tenths of a cent per gallon higher than those reported to the *WPI*. That may be due to definitional differences. The FEA-P302 does not differentiate between sales to commercial accounts and jobbers. Both are reported as wholesale and have been compared to *WPI* jobber sales for the purposes of this analysis. Platt's survey reports posted prices from regional refineries without regard to customer. Therefore, no prices are available from *Platt's* for regular gasoline sales to jobbers.

## Summary

In the absence of large volumes of third party transactions, the development of a transfer pricing system based on a market price requires access to published prices that purport to mirror market transactions.

The company interviews in chapter 5 pointed out that most vertically integrated companies do not sell large percentages of their refinery output on the third party market. Therefore, the authors reviewed existing published price series that might serve as a basis for a transfer price.

Only three have possible relevance to the DOE. They are: *Platt's Oil Price Service* and *Oil Price Handbook,* BLSs *Wholesale Price Indexes for Petroleum Products* and the DOEs FEA–P302. Each has specific strengths and weaknesses. *Platt's Oilgram Price Service* is reviewed daily by oil company executives and oil analysts. Its strengths are its timeliness and range of products and market locations. As a general monitoring device for oil companies, it is a useful tool. Its chief weakness is its inability to be validated. *Platt's* selects companies for telephone surveys. The surveyed companies choose which sales to report. The development of functional profit statements based on selective data is not wise.

The two published price series over which the federal government has control, the *WPI* and FEA–P302, do not recognize the complex distribution systems that have developed for petroleum products. The gasoline distribution system, described in figure 5–1, points out the possible transaction points at which a sale could be made. Gasoline prices vary depending on the point in the distribution chain at which the sale is made. Both the *WPI* and FEA–P302 collapse the alternative distribution points into wholesale and retail, although *WPI* does report separately sales to end users.

Figure 8–1 is summarized in figure 8–2, illustrating the range of price variation that results from the differing data collection techniques, product definitions, and transaction points used by the three published price series.

For gasoline (figures 8–1 and 8–2), the outer bounds of the prices for dealer tank wagon sales and for sales to jobbers are never more than 1 cent apart. Gasoline is the most clearly defined of all petroleum products, which accounts for the similarity of the prices.

Using published price series as the basis for transfer prices impacts on financial profitability analysis in two ways. The variance of the price for each product can affect the total revenues credited to the refining function and charged to the marketing function. The impact of variances in gasoline prices will be discussed in the next section.

The combined variances should also be considered. Even though the variation in price for each product may be small, the sum of the variations could have a profound effect on the profitability of each function.

## Notes

1. *Platt's Oilgram Price Service* (New York, McGraw-Hill, Inc., Vol. 56, No. 48, March 10, 1978, Page 5-A.

2. *Platt's Oil Price Handbook,* (New York, McGraw-Hill, Inc., 1951), 53rd ed, p. 4.

3. *Federal Energy Guidelines.* FEA-P302-M-1.

4. Ibid.

5. Ibid.

# Sensitivity of Functional Profitability to Transfer Price Method

The following section calculates functional profitability using four alternative transfer pricing systems. Major shifts in functional profitability result from using these systems. The purpose of this analysis is to highlight how sensitive functional profitability is to slight changes in price.

Two fundamental considerations must be understood when reading the analysis:

1. Only one variable, the transfer price of gasoline, is changed. All other products are transferred at average per gallon costs.

2. Product and functional cost allocations used in this analysis are for illustrative purposes only. The methodology used is not recommended for use by public policy makers and serves only as a useful way of viewing variances in profitability caused by applying different transfer price. No conclusions should be reached regarding absolute profits of any one segment. This analysis focuses on variances in revenue, leaving costs constant. If the intricacies of cost allocations are also taken into account, even greater fluctuations in profits may occur.

Four transfer pricing systems are of potential use for developing industrywide functional profitability statements. This chapter describes each system, and then calculates functional profitability using the system's transfer price formula. The four systems are:

1. Cost plus return on investment
2. Company's own transfer pricing system
3. Company's third party sales
4. Published price series

Both the third and fourth systems are market-based transfer pricing systems.

Several of the systems were recommended by oil industry analysts. Others are market-based, relying on company data or published price series. These latter systems attempt to reflect what the marketplace transactions would have been if the oil companies were not vertically integrated.

The emphasis of the financial analysis completed here is the impact of different transfer prices on the measurement of each function's performance. The performance remains unchanged; only the perception changes.

The base financial statements for 1974, showing refining and marketing as one combined profit center, are given in tables 9-1 and 9-2. They are derived from the 1974 Chase Manhattan Energy Data Base which contains financial

**Table 9-1**
**1974 Functional Pro Forma Balance Sheet for the Domestic Operations of 18 Major Petroleum Companies**
*(millions of dollars)*

| | Production | Transportation | Refining | Marketing | Other | Total |
|---|---|---|---|---|---|---|
| *Assets* | | | | | | |
| Cash and marketable securities | $ 2,000 | $ 500 | $ 1,600 | $ 2,000 | $ 494 | $ 6,594 |
| Accounts receivable | 875 | 500 | 3,800 | 6,000 | 500 | 11,675 |
| Inventory | 800 | 0 | 4,942 | 3,050 | 8 | 8,800 |
| Current assets | $ 3,675 | $ 1,000 | $10,342 | $11,050 | $ 1,002 | $ 27,069 |
| Investment and advances | 500 | 100 | 0 | 400 | 1,005 | 2,005 |
| Gross fixed assets | 46,819 | 6,505 | 21,060 | 11,508 | 3,359 | 89,251 |
| Reserves for depreciation | (22,142) | (2,864) | (9,796) | (3,792) | (1,126) | (39,720) |
| Net fixed assets | $24,677 | $ 3,641 | $11,264 | $ 7,716 | $ 2,233 | $ 49,531 |
| Other assets | 841 | 124 | 370 | 260 | 86 | 1,681 |
| Total assets | $ 29,693 | $ 4,865 | $21,976 | $19,426 | $ 4,326 | $ 80,286 |
| *Liabilities* | | | | | | |
| Accounts payable | $ 715 | $ 395 | $ 1,925 | $ 5,000 | $ 385 | $ 8,420 |
| Notes payable | 10 | 5 | 1,500 | 970 | 15 | 2,500 |
| Other | 500 | 100 | 2,178 | 1,500 | 100 | 4,378 |
| Current liabilities | $ 1,225 | $ 500 | $ 5,603 | $ 7,470 | $ 500 | $ 15,298 |
| Long-term debt | 1,500 | 1,500 | 6,150 | 3,405 | 1,501 | 14,056 |
| Other liabilities | 4,000 | 280 | 860 | 590 | 169 | 5,899 |
| Net worth excluding preferred | 22,858 | 2,585 | 9,201 | 7,961 | 2,154 | 44,759 |
| Preferred stock | 110 | 0 | 162 | 0 | 2 | 274 |
| Net worth including preferred | $ 22,968 | $ 2,585 | $ 9,363 | $ 7,961 | $ 2,156 | $ 45,033 |
| Total liabilities and net worth | $ 29,693 | $ 4,865 | $21,976 | $19,426 | $ 4,326 | $ 80,286 |
| Working capital (current assets–current liabilities) | 2,450 | 500 | 4,739 | 3,580 | 502 | 11,771 |
| Net fixed assets | 24,677 | 3,641 | 11,264 | 7,716 | 2,233 | 49,531 |
| Total investment for ROI Purposes | $ 27,127 | $ 4,141 | $16,003 | $11,296 | $ 2,735 | $ 61,302 |

**Table 9-2**
**1974 Functional Pro Forma Income Statement for the Domestic Operations of 18 Major Petroleum Companies**
*(millions of dollars)*

| | *Production* | *Transportation* | *Refining* | *Marketing* | *Other* | *Total* |
|---|---|---|---|---|---|---|
| Gross revenue | $16,700 | $1,020 | $ 0 | $72,240 | $3,000 | $92,960 |
| Product costs }<br>Operating costs } | 3,200 } | 500 } | 45,350<br>4,400 | 0<br>15,050 | } 1,999 | } 70,499 |
| Taxes other than<br>  income taxes | 1,700 | 0 | 644 | 200 | 0 | 2,544 |
| Write-offs | 3,000 | 200 | 1,300 | 1,250 | 250 | 6,000 |
| Interest and other | 125 | 125 | 525 | 300 | 125 | 1,200 |
| Pretax income | $ 8,675 | $ 195 | $3,221 | | $ 626 | $12,717 |
| Income taxes | 2,725 | 95 | 1,546 | | 325 | 4,691 |
| Net income, before<br>  extraordinary items | $ 5,950 | $ 100 | $1,675 | | $ 301 | $ 8,026 |
| ROI[a] | 22% | 2% | 6% | | 11% | 13% |
| Total investment<br>  (from Table 9-1) | $27,127 | $4,141 | $16,003 | $11,296 | $2,735 | $61,302 |

[a]Return = net income after tax
investment = net fixed assets + net working capital.

data on eighteen major petroleum companies. Concern for strict allocation of costs, assets, and liabilities was set aside in order to focus on the interaction of the refining and marketing functions. All allocations were made by Chase.

For each of the following financial statements, only one variable, the transfer price of gasoline, is changed. Transfer prices are calculated for gasoline, using the formula on which each transfer pricing system is based. All other products are transferred at average per gallon cost. The transfer price is applied to the estimated output of gasoline during 1974 to determine how the same performance would be viewed depending on how the functional profits are calculated.

The base cost assumptions are that:

The refining functions of the eighteen combined companies processed 5 billion barrels of crude oil (210,000 million gallons) in 1974. (Official 1974 DOE estimates from Bureau of Mines were approximately 4.9 billion barrels.)

Gasoline represented 47 percent (98,700 million gallons) of all refinery output. The other products represented 53 percent (111,300 million gallons) of all refinery output.

All of the refinery output was transferred to the marketing function where additional processing and marketing costs were incurred. The products were sold by marketing for a total of $72,240 million. Revenue calculations are detailed in table 9-3.

Operating costs for the refining function averaged $.88 a barrel in 1974, based on Chase estimates. Total refinery operating costs = ($.88/barrel) (5,000 million barrels) = $4,400 million.

Crude oil costs for the refining function averaged $9.07 a barrel, according

**Table 9-3**
**Detail Calculation of the Average per Gallon Revenue Received by the Marketing Function**

| Product and Type of Sale | (1) 1974 Price per Gallon[a] | (2) Percent Sold Through Distribution Channel | (3) Yield | (4) Weighted Average [(1) × (3)] |
|---|---|---|---|---|
| Gasoline–all grades combined | | | | |
| Jobber (wholesale) | $.282[b] | .373[c] | .175[d] | $.049 |
| Dealer tank wagon (wholesale) | .320[e] | .116[c] | .055[d] | .018 |
| Bulk sales (end user) | .320[e] | .082[c] | .039[d] | 0.12 |
| Company-controlled stations (Retail) | .421[f] | .429[c] | .202[d] | .085 |
| | | | .47 | $.164 |
| Distillates (heating oil) | .343[g] | | .22[h] | .075 |
| Residual fuel | .266[i] | | .08[h] | .021 |
| Other products (jet fuel, etc.) | .365[i] | | .23[h] | .084 |
| | | | | Total $.344/gallon |

Total marketing revenues = $.344/gallon × 210,000 million gallons = $72,240 million

[a]Multiple data sources were required because no one source contained all the required prices. All prices, regardless of when they were published, are for 1974.
[b]DOE's Monthly Energy Review, August, 1977, page 67.
[c]Findings and Views Concerning the Exemption of Motor Gasoline from the Mandatory Petroleum Allocation and Price Regulations, September, 1977, page 63.
[d]Yield for gasoline = (.47) (% sold through distribution channel)
[e]Platt's 1975 Oil Price Handbook, page 106.
[f]DOE's Monthly Energy Review, August, 1977, page 56.
[g]DOE's Monthly Energy Review, August, 1977, page 41.
[h]Findings and Views Concerning the Exemption of Motor Gasoline from the Mandatory Petroleum Allocation and Price Regulations, September, 1977, page 26.
[i]DOE's Monthly Energy Review, August, 1977, page 67.

to DOEs 1974 *Monthly Energy Review.* Total refinery product costs =
($9.07/barrel) (5,000 million barrels) = $45,350 million.

Operating costs for the marketing function averaged $3.01 per barrel, according to 1974 Chase data. Total operating costs for marketing function
= ($3.01/barrel) (5,000 million barrels) = $15,050 million.

The tax rate for all nonproducing functions in 1974 was assumed to be 48 percent.

Total fully absorbed refining costs average $.249/gallon ($52,219 million)
÷ (210,000 million gallons) = $.249/gallon.

Total allocated costs for refining gasoline = ($.249) × (98,700 million gallons) = $24,576 million.

All nongasoline products were transferred from the refining function to the marketing function at cost. Total transfer value for nongasoline products was $27,643 million. ($52,219 million - $24,576 million = $27,643 million).

The base financial statements, showing refining and marketing as one combined profit center, are given in tables 9-1 and 9-2.

## Cost-Plus Predetermined Return on Investment as a Transfer Pricing System

One system for calculating the transfer price of products that move from the refinery unit to the marketing unit is to take the cost of each product and add a predetermined ROI to the cost base. The three variables in the transfer price formula are costs, ROI, and investment base, where costs are the standard, fully absorbed costs for each product. The transfer price equation would be:

*Transfer Price = Cost + (Rate of Return) (Investment Base)*

Assuming that all nongasoline products are transferred from the refining function to the marketing function at cost ($27,643 million), tables 9-4 and 9-5 illustrate the impact on functional profitability of changing one variable in the transfer pricing formula. In table 9-4, the refining function receives a 6 percent rate of return on its investment. That is the rate of return for the combined refining and marketing segments. In table 9-5, refining receives a 10 percent rate of return, the average ROA (return on assets) for petroleum companies in 1974.[1] At a 6 percent rate of return (table 9-4), the marketing function segment of the oil industry appears to be twice as profitable as the refining segment and earns three times the return on its investment. At a 10 percent rate of return (table 9-5), the segments are equally profitable.

**Table 9-4**
**1974 Functional Pro Forma Income Statement for the Domestic Operations of 18 Major Petroleum Companies**
*(millions of dollars)*

| | Production | Transportation | Refining | Marketing | Other | Total |
|---|---|---|---|---|---|---|
| Gross revenue | $16,700 | $1,020 | $53,179[b] | $72,240 | $3,000 | $146,139 |
| Product costs | 3,200 | 500 | 45,350 | 53,179 | 1,999 | 123,678 |
| Operating costs | | | 4,400 | 15,050 | | |
| Taxes other than income taxes | 1,700 | 0 | 644 | 200 | 0 | 2,544 |
| Write-offs | 3,000 | 200 | 1,300 | 1,250 | 250 | 6,000 |
| Interest and other | 125 | 125 | 525 | 300 | 125 | 1,200 |
| Pretax income | $ 8,675 | $ 195 | $ 960 | $ 2,261 | $ 626 | $ 12,717 |
| Income taxes | 2,725 | 95 | 461 | 1,085 | 325 | 4,691 |
| Net income, before extraordinary items | $ 5,950 | $ 100 | $ 499 | $ 1,176 | $ 301 | $ 8,026 |
| ROI[a] | 22% | 2% | 3% | 10% | 11% | 13% |
| Total investment (from Table 9-1) | $27,127 | $4,141 | $16,003 | $11,296 | $2,735 | $61,302 |

Refining revenues derived from transfer pricing system based on cost plus predetermined ROI of 6%

[a]Return = net income after tax
investment = net fixed assets + net working capital.

[b]Total revenues from gasoline = $24,576 + [(.06)(16,003)] = $25,536
Total revenues from all other products (at cost) = 27,643
$53,179

**Table 9-5**
**1974 Functional Pro Forma Income Statement for the Domestic Operations of 18 Major Petroleum Companies**
*(millions of dollars)*

| | Production | Transportation | Refining | Marketing | Other | Total |
|---|---|---|---|---|---|---|
| Gross revenue | $16,700 | $1,020 | $53,819 | $72,240 | $3,000 | $146,779 |
| Product costs | 3,200 | 500 | 45,350 | 53,819 | 1,999 | 124,318 |
| Operating costs | | | 4,400 | 15,050 | | |
| Taxes other than income taxes | 1,700 | 0 | 644 | 200 | 0 | 2,544 |
| Write-offs | 3,000 | 200 | 1,300 | 1,250 | 250 | 6,000 |
| Interest and other | 125 | 125 | 525 | 300 | 125 | 1,200 |
| Pretax income | $ 8,675 | $ 195 | $ 1,600 | $ 1,621 | $ 626 | $ 12,717 |
| Income taxes | 2,725 | 95 | 768 | 778 | 325 | 4,691 |
| Net income, before extraordinary items | $ 5,950 | $ 100 | $ 832 | $ 843 | $ 301 | $ 8,026 |
| ROI[a] | 22% | 2% | 5% | 7% | 11% | 13% |
| Total investment (from Table 9-1) | $27,127 | $4,141 | $16,003 | $11,296 | $2,735 | $ 61,302 |

Refining revenues derived from transfer pricing system based on cost plus predetermined ROI of 10%

[a]Return = net income after tax

investment = net fixed assets + net working capital.

[b]Total revenues from gasoline = ($24,576) + [(.10)(16,003)] = $26,176
                                    = 27,643
                                    $53,819

There are two major problems with using a cost plus predetermined rate of return for an industry-wide transfer pricing system. The first is that someone would need to determine both a reasonable rate of return for refineries and an appropriate investment base.

Second, a transfer price based on cost plus a predetermined ROI provides no incremental information over cost data alone. Cost data for refinery units will be available from the DOEs Financial Reporting System.

Not only does a uniform transfer fee pricing system not provide incremental information, it creates a false sense of increased knowledge that may lead to inappropriate decisions. Changing the rate of return or including different assets in the investment base leads to different pictures of the activities and relationships of the refinery and marketing units. The activities themselves are not changing, only the numbers used to describe the relationships.

### Company's Own Transfer Pricing System

Another alternative system that has been suggested is that each company report the transfer price it uses for internal reporting purposes. This method would allow policy makers to implement a refinery/marketing split quickly and save oil companies the time and money required to establish a second transfer pricing system for federal reporting purposes only. Two problems surface immediately. First, some companies do not use transfer pricing. For these companies, a default system would be required. That is, a transfer pricing system would be created for companies that do not have an internal system. If a default system must be designated, no benefit is gained from allowing each company to use its own system.

Second, as pointed out in chapter 5, each company designs its transfer price system to meet its special needs. The system may not be appropriate for public policy. For example, Company C uses a cost-based transfer price for products, believing that the refinery, as a factory, should not share in the profits of products sold by marketing. The refining unit, therefore, would show no profits if Company C's transfer price data were submitted, unaltered, to the government.

One of the major challenges of developing an industry-wide transfer pricing system is to obtain comparable data. If each company is allowed to use its own transfer pricing system, which has been designed for internal use and reflects the organizational structure peculiar to the company, comparing the results may lead to incorrect conclusions. The actual product transfer points vary from company to company, as illustrated in chapter 5. The definition of and range of responsibilities for refining and marketing also differ, with refining representing not only processing activities in Company C, but also including industrial sales in Company E.

By comparing the income ($499 million) of the refining unit in table 9-4 with the income ($0) of the refining unit in table 9-6, one might conclude that

**Table 9-6**
**1974 Functional Pro Forma Income Statement for the Domestic Operations of 18 Major Petroleum Companies**
*(millions of dollars)*

| | Production | Transportation | Refining | Marketing | Other | Total |
|---|---|---|---|---|---|---|
| Gross revenue | $16,700 | $1,020 | $52,219 | $72,240 | $3,000 | $145,179 |
| Product costs | 3,200 | 500 | 45,350 | 52,219 | 1,999 | 122,718 |
| Operating costs | | | 4,400 | 15,050 | | |
| Taxes other than income taxes | 1,700 | 0 | 644 | 200 | 0 | 2,544 |
| Write-offs | 3,000 | 200 | 1,300 | 1,250 | 250 | 6,000 |
| Interest and other | 125 | 125 | 525 | 300 | 125 | 1,200 |
| Pretax income | $ 8,675 | $ 195 | $ 0 | $ 3,221 | $ 626 | $ 12,717 |
| Income taxes | 2,725 | 95 | 0 | 1,546 | 325 | 4,691 |
| Net income, before extraordinary items | $ 5,950 | $ 100 | $ 0 | $ 1,675 | $ 301 | $ 8,026 |
| ROI[a] | 22% | 2% | 0% | 15% | 11% | 13% |
| Total investment (from Table 9-1) | $27,127 | $4,141 | $16,003 | $11,296 | $2,735 | $ 61,302 |

Refining revenues derived from transfer pricing system based on cost
[a] Return = net income after tax
investment = net fixed assets + net working capital.
[b] Total revenues from gasoline        = $24,576
Total revenues from all other products =   27,643
                                          $52,219

the latter unit is inefficient. But these two statements represent two different ways of looking at the operations of the same refining unit. Comparisons of different companies using different transfer pricing systems may similarly lead to erroneous conclusions.

## Market-Based Transfer Pricing System

The other two transfer pricing systems are market-based. A market-based transfer pricing system requires access to actual third party transaction information. The information is derived from actual third party sales made by the company's refining unit or from published price series. The three published price series discussed here are *Platt's Oilgram Price Service* and *Handbook*, the Bureau of Labor Statistics *WPI* and the Department of Energy's P-302. All three are described in detail in chapter 8.

All market-based transfer pricing systems attempt to reflect what price the product would have been sold for (or purchased for) if the two business units had been individual companies. The system that comes closest to that concept is one that is based on actual third party sales that the company has made.

Both Companies E and F use this system, as described in chapter 5. Sometimes adjustments are made to the third party sales price to reflect credit arrangements, transportation costs, or other specific features that make the internal transfer slightly different from an external sale.

The formula for a transfer price based on third party sales is:

Transfer Price = Third-party sales price for the same product in the same market area ± adjustment factor

The usefulness and accuracy of this system are dependent on how closely the third-party sale price resembles the internal transfer. As the volume of products transferred from the refining unit to the marketing unit increases, it is more difficult to use actual third-party sales prices as the transfer price. There are two reasons for this. First, large quantities of internal transfers normally indicate that the refining unit is a function providing manufacturing services for the marketing unit. Business units known as function are process oriented and do not have sufficient responsibilities to make profit analysis meaningful. Key profit-related decisions such as how to distribute the refinery output are not made at a functional level.

Second, from a practical point of view, if only a small percentage of the refinery output is sold to third parties, the sales normally represent a problem with coordination between the refining and marketing units. If the refining unit is producing more than the marketing unit can use, the corporation may determine that selling gasoline on the third party market is more profitable than holding the excess in inventory until such time as the marketing function can sell the products. The price received in the third party market may be a spot price and not representative of the price at which the company would sell the product on a long-term basis to a regular customer, such as the marketing function.

In table 9–7, the price that the marketing function receives for gasoline distributed to wholesale jobbers ($.282/gallon) is applied to all gasoline sales. The result is that the refining segment earns all the profits, while the marketing segment loses $19 million.

### Published Price Series as Basis of Market Price

The contrast between the two segments becomes even more marked when any of the published price series are used as the basis for the gasoline transfer price. That formula is:

$$\text{Transfer Price} = \text{Published price} \pm \text{adjustment factor}$$

Because only the ranges of variation are of interest here, no adjustments have been made to any of the published price series.

The national average dealer tank wagon (wholesale) price reported in *Platt's* in 1974 was $.320 a gallon (see table 9–3.). The total variation among *Platt's*, *WPI* and EIA Form P-302 never varied by more than 1 cent in the time period studied. Table 9–8 illustrates the effect on profits and ROI when all gasoline is transferred at the *Platt's* published price of $.320. In table 9–9, the price has dropped 1 cent, to $.310 per gallon, representing the lower bounds of *WPI* or EIA P-302 price. The upper bounds of $.330 per gallon would show even more dramatic losses for marketing and were, therefore, not calculated.

### Summary

Although individual companies conduct functional profitability analyses, they are not desirable as a means to assess the economic performance of the energy industry. Collecting data to measure functional profitability may provide some incremental information for addressing the issues of the competitive nature of the energy industry, the impact of federal regulatory policy, and the development of energy resources. However, the analysis that results from conducting functional profitability is based on allocated cost assumptions, does not recognize individual organizational differences among companies, and relies on transfer prices that camouflage the importance of vertical integration, a dominant feature of the industry.

Tables 9–4 through 9–9 have illustrated the impact on function profitability

**Table 9-7**
**1974 Functional Pro Forma Income Statement for the Domestic Operations of 18 Major Petroleum Companies**
*(millions of dollars)*

| | Production | Transportation | Refining | Marketing | Other | Total |
|---|---|---|---|---|---|---|
| Gross revenue | $16,700 | $1,020 | $55,476[b] | $72,240 | $3,000 | $148,436 |
| Product costs | 3,200 | 500 | 45,350 | 55,476 | 1,999 | 125,975 |
| Operating costs | | | 4,400 | 15,050 | | |
| Taxes other than income taxes | 1,700 | 0 | 644 | 200 | 0 | 2,544 |
| Write-offs | 3,000 | 200 | 1,300 | 1,250 | 250 | 6,000 |
| Interest and other | 125 | 125 | 525 | 300 | 125 | 1,200 |
| Pretax income | $ 8,675 | $ 195 | $ 3,257 | $ (36) | $ 626 | $ 12,717 |
| Income taxes | 2,725 | 95 | 1,563 | (17) | 325 | 4,691 |
| Net income, before extraordinary items | $ 5,950 | $ 100 | $ 1,694 | $ (19) | $ 301 | $ 8,026 |
| ROI[a] | 22% | 2% | 11% | 0% | 11% | 13% |
| Total investment (from Table 9-1) | $27,127 | $4,141 | $16,003 | $11,296 | $2,735 | $ 61,302 |

Refining revenues derived from transfer pricing system based on wholesale jobber price

[a]Return = net income after tax
investment = net fixed assets + net working capital.

[b]Total revenues from gasoline = ($.282/gallon) (98,700) = $27,833
$$\text{Total revenues from all other products} = \frac{27,643}{\$55,476}$$

**Table 9-8**
**1974 Functional Pro Forma Income Statement for the Domestic Operations of 18 Major Petroleum Companies**
*(millions of dollars)*

| | Production | Transportation | Refining | Marketing | Other | Total |
|---|---|---|---|---|---|---|
| Gross revenue | $16,700 | $1,020 | $59,227[b] | $72,240 | $3,000 | $152,187 |
| Product costs | 3,200 | 500 | 45,350 | 59,227 | 1,999 | 129,726 |
| Operating costs | | | 4,400 | 15,050 | | |
| Taxes other than income taxes | 1,700 | 0 | 644 | 200 | 0 | 2,544 |
| Write-offs | 3,000 | 200 | 1,300 | 1,250 | 250 | 6,000 |
| Interest and other | 125 | 125 | 525 | 300 | 125 | 1,200 |
| Pretax income | $ 8,675 | $ 195 | $ 7,008 | $ (3,787) | $ 626 | $ 12,717 |
| Income taxes | 2,725 | 95 | 3,364 | (1,818) | 325 | 4,691 |
| Net income, before extraordinary items | $ 5,950 | $ 100 | $ 3,644 | $ (1,969) | $ 301 | $ 8,026 |
| ROI[a] | 22% | 2% | 23% | 0% | 11% | 13% |
| Total investment (from Table 9-1) | $27,127 | $4,141 | $16,003 | $11,296 | $2,735 | $ 61,302 |

Refining revenues derived from transfer pricing system based on Platt's wholesale price

[a] Return = net income after tax
investment = net fixed assets + net working capital.

[b] Total revenues from gasoline = ($.320)(98,700) = $31,584
$$= \underline{27,643}$$
$$\$59,227$$

**Table 9-9**
**1974 Functional Pro Forma Income Statement for the Domestic Operations of 18 Major Petroleum Companies**
*(millions of dollars)*

| | Production | Transportation | Refining | Marketing | Other | Total |
|---|---|---|---|---|---|---|
| Gross revenue | $16,700 | $1,020 | $58,240[b] | $72,240 | $3,000 | $151,200 |
| Product costs | 3,200 | 500 | 45,350 | 58,240 | 1,999 | 128,739 |
| Operating costs | | | 4,400 | 15,050 | | |
| Taxes other than income taxes | 1,700 | 0 | 644 | 200 | 0 | 2,544 |
| Write-offs | 3,000 | 200 | 1,300 | 1,250 | 250 | 6,000 |
| Interest and other | 125 | 125 | 525 | 300 | 125 | 1,200 |
| Pretax income | $ 8,675 | $ 195 | $ 6,021 | $ (2,800) | $ 626 | $ 12,717 |
| Income taxes | 2,725 | 95 | 2,890 | (1,344) | 325 | 4,691 |
| Net income, before extraordinary items | $ 5,950 | $ 100 | $ 3,131 | $ (1,456) | $ 301 | $ 8,026 |
| ROI[a] | 22% | 2% | 20% | 0% | 11% | 13% |
| Total investment (from Table 9-1) | $27,127 | $4,141 | $16,003 | $11,296 | $2,735 | $ 61,302 |

Refining revenues derived from transfer pricing system based on 1 cent below Platt's wholesale price

[a]Return = net income after tax
investment = net fixed assets + net working capital.

[b]Total revenues from gasoline = (.310)(98,700) = $30,597
Total revenues from all other products = 27,643
$58,240

measures of using different transfer pricing systems. The profits for the refining function ranged from $0 to $3,664 million, and the ROI varied from 0 percent to 23 percent. The profits for the marketing function ranged from a loss of $1,969 million to a profit of $1,675 million, and the ROI varied from no return to 15 percent. The combined after-tax profits were always $1,675 million, and the combined ROI was always 6 percent.

All of the transfer pricing systems described here contain serious flaws that compromise their validity as an industry-wide system.

A transfer pricing system based on costs plus predetermined ROI investment provides no incremental information over the cost data already being collected by the federal government.

If each company is allowed to use its own transfer pricing system, the results will not be comparable due to structural differences among companies. In addition, a government transfer pricing system would still need to be created for those companies that do not have their own systems.

A transfer price system based on third party sales provides accurate data only if integrated companies sell a large percentage of their refinery output on the third party market. Most of them do not.

No published price series collects auditable prices for the broad range of products, customers, and markets that must be included in a transfer pricing system. Although an adjustment factor may be used to compensate for differences between published prices and internal company transfers, the profit levels for the two functions are very sensitive to error.

The *performance* of the two units never varied, only the methods used to view the performance. The swings in profitability result from small per gallon changes in the transfer price. The large volumes and narrow per gallon product profit margins account for the large variances.

Specifically, the total before-tax profits for the refining and marketing segments combined are $3,221 million (table 9-2). With total annual output equaling 210,000 million gallons, the profit margin per gallon for the combined refining and marketing business units is $.015 ($3,221 million ÷ 210,000 million gallons). To evaluate the performance of each function or segment of the industry, the $.015 has to be allocated between the two functions. None of the transfer pricing systems available to public policy makers can be sufficiently fine-tuned to ensure that the allocation of profits is appropriate.

At best, functional profit statements allow public policy makers to ask questions such as:

Do functional profits in integrated companies differ (or not differ) in magnitude from profits of independent companies?

Why do differences exist (or not exist)?

The reasons for the differences or lack of differences lead analysts to the real questions that must be addressed. These relate to the competitive environment of the industry, the development of domestic energy resources, and the impact of government regulations.

## Notes

1. Shyam Sunder, *Oil Industry Profits* (American Enterprise Institute for Public Policy Research, Washington, D.C., 1977), p. 27.

# Part V
# Conclusions

# 10 The Regulatory Value of Performance Information

The logic of the arguments in the first nine chapters must now be applied to one question: What performance information should be collected in order to analyze the workability of competition in the U.S. petroleum industry?

As related in chapter 1, the political environment of the petroleum industry has an emotionally charged history. Performance evaluations have often been the process through which political judgments and economic reforms could be facilitated or suppressed. Given the urgency of the issues, analysts have had to settle for the "least worst" data they could find. The data that were available came from traditional sources: external reporting, trade associations, industry data services, and government surveys.

Traditional data sources have had their own strengths and weaknesses relative to the purposes for which they were collected. The remedy for the weaknesses of disparate data sources is the development of a single, consistent source of data on the industry. Paradoxically, this chapter will conclude that this solution is fraught with problems of its own.

The distinguishing feature of the arguments articulated in this book is the commitment to one viewpoint, that of the public policymaker. Public policy decisions in petroleum require information that differs materially from other data collection efforts. Previously, information has not been collected for the public policymaker. The FRS represents the initial attempt to do so. The focused perspective of public policy renders traditional sources of data inadequate. This book has reviewed the various sources and uses of data. To choose among alternative data sets, an analytical framework is necessary. Drawing on our observations in the previous chapters, several types of analytical questions have appeared repeatedly, suggesting the content of an analytical process for evaluating performance information. The questions are arrayed along the dimension of their source versus use orientation. Figure 10-1 displays these questions in the form of a decision tree. The source versus use dimension is displayed from left to right.

Explanations of the questions follow:

1. *Availability of information.* This is the basic source question. If data are already available, they are likely to involve lower costs of collection. If data are not available, the logical question is whether they can be developed at a reasonable cost.

2. *Consistency of information.* Are the different sources of information supplying data in the same way, both among sources and over time? Also, are

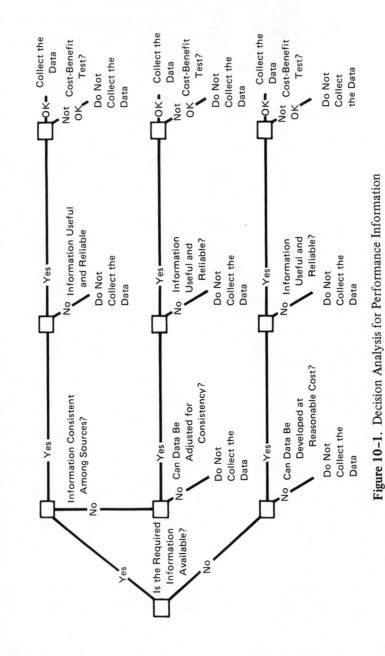

**Figure 10-1.** Decision Analysis for Performance Information

different data items from a given source comparable? If data inconsistency exists, various techniques (sampling, simulation, and auditing) can possibly be employed to adjust the data.

3. *Usefulness and reliability of information.* Do the data relate to the hypotheses to be tested? Can one rely on the data to discern the validity of hypotheses?

4. *Cost-benefit test.* Is the information obtained worth the cost of collecting it? What is the distribution of benefits and costs?

To understand the value of information systems, it is logical to start analyses by answering the four questions in the reverse order of that listed above. This allows one to perform a preposterior analysis (as mentioned in chapter 1). The question becomes: If I had the right data, what could I conclude from it?" Most of this book has dealt with questions of this type. In contrast, most performance measurement in petroleum has historically dealt with source questions first. After obtaining the most readily available and consistent data, people have applied it without sufficient regard to its potential for shedding light on useful questions or of the costs associated with the use or misuses of the information.

## Usefulness and Reliability

Analyzing the usefulness question first, it has been concluded in this book that an economic framework is necessary for evaluating the workability of competition. We can, however, take the analysis one step further. Having cast doubt on the ability of the structure-conduct-performance model to offer precise standards for evaluating performance data, the reliability of annual performance data, for example, must be questioned. Would a 10 percent variation in some measures, after adjusting for historical explanatory variables, provide sufficient cause for a policy adjustment by DOE, a change in the behavior of potential entrants, or some other significant use of the data? At the present state of knowledge, the answer is negative. However, if quality data has been the most significant obstacle, the answer could be positive.

The foregoing suggests that performance data might properly be evaluated within the context of specific regulatory (or deregulatory) actions. Performance data could then be compared to the predicted consequences of the regulatory actions. The data to be collected must allow one to gauge the likely effect of the regulatory action. Such data might be nonexistent (such as the rate of resource development under a regime of deregulated petroleum prices).

Consider the early 1979 White House proposals to decontrol crude oil prices and impose an excess profits tax. Ideally it would be useful to compare petroleum industry performance with and without the policy changes. Only then might a meaningful comparison result. We say "might" because data source considerations could obfuscate the true effects. The analysis will actually be a comparison of predicted performance with actual postchange results.

The benefits from using quality economic data—as might ideally be collected by the FRS—depend critically on the reliability of the prediction methodology. Typically, analysts depend on their prior hypotheses about the industry to interpret the data. Given such a classical statistics methodology, only markedly different results can overturn the prior hypotheses.

Ideological opponents, holding disparate views on the workability of competition, do not simply disagree on the values of some common set of indicators. Procompany advocates emphasize the efficiencies of vertical integration and control. Anticompany advocates emphasize the shared monopoly of the majors, the barriers to entry, and other hypotheses stated in chapter 1. A set of performance data is unlikely ever to settle the debate among these groups because the data will never reveal which of the sets of variables are more important.

Having demonstrated the unlikely possibility of a data base being able to settle the great debates about industry competition, we still can make some positive statements about the specific value of economic performance measures. Important questions about the impact of regulation and the magnitude of changes in key variables of structure, conduct, and performance are necessary to establish a very basic level of communication in the industry. For example, regulatory hearings require reliable data.

A potentially important benefit of an industry data base is information to enhance competition. Potential entrants, nonintegrated firms, and even major, integrated firms would have better information on which to base their strategy. In a highly integrated industry, the absence of information is a vital competitive impediment; indeed, it is often a motivation to integrate!

## Consistency

Several factors play a role in an evaluation of consistency of data collected from petroleum companies. Parts II and IV presented these factors in great detail. Summarily:

1. Corporate organization is important in influencing the data that might be supplied. Because structures vary by company and industry subsegment and over time, the meaning of data will also vary.

2. Functional profitability is impractical as a measure of the performance of individual vertical functions. The complexity of the reasons for integration and the differences in corporate organization render the development of functional profit data an undesirable venture. The resulting data would not be interpretable in any consistent fashion.

3. Transfer pricing, an important element of functional profitability analysis, does not offer a simple solution to the performance evaluation problem.

There does not seem to exist a useful way of adjusting petroleum industry data to facilitate consistency. The alternative of developing a uniform method of dealing with all the data collection problems—assuming identical organization, transfer prices, accounting practices, and prices—is a solution that defines away the most meaningful problems. The objective of an economic evaluation of the industry would be to understand the relative virtues of different corporate practices. While a uniform system of collection might fulfill certain requirements of accounting theory and might make the problem of source availability simple, it would not satisfy the requisites of an economics-based system at all.

## Availability

The availability of data affects the cost of collection, just as the usefulness of data affects the benefits. Our survey of market price information in chapter 8 and our discussion of different organizational structures and, therefore, different practices on costs, suggest that readily available data are not appropriate in large quantities. Certain selected data are available from corporations and many are already collected by DOE. These data can provide clues about the performance of petroleum companies, but they cannot tell the whole story.

The ability to develop new sources of data through a uniformly imposed set of accounting standards has already been discussed. Another avenue offers more promise. Special-purpose studies of economic questions about the industry—scale economies, transactions costs, and distribution practices—could be a valuable supplement to the stock of knowledge on the industry. A time series of such studies could be enormously valuable in making policy decisions.

The development of special-purpose sources of data to integrate with the most desirable uses of data is an exciting prospect. In that way, the state of knowledge about the economics of the industry and the complex reasons for heterogeneity within the industry can serve as a foundation for highly focused research and debate. The opposite approach of making some simplifying assumptions about industry behavior and ignoring important differences among companies to facilitate the development of a large data base is distinctly less promising.

## Reflections

One topic that deserves reflection is the economics of performance measurement. In the short history of industrial organization, very little has been written on the positive theories of performance measurement. Typically, an economist develops hypotheses, looks for data, tests the hypotheses, and then complains about the inadequacy of the data as an excuse for poor predictive performance.

Economics in general, and industrial organization in particular, serve as the foundation for the multidimensionality of performance as a concept. The theoretical tradition is a rich one. Very little effort has been made to apply the foundation in a definition of what data might be collected. This book has attempted to accomplish that task for the petroleum industry by integrating economics with the messy details of accounting, management, and regulation. The task was made easy by the ready supply of overly simplistic approaches in current debate and practice. We hope that those who follow in our footsteps can offer more positive direction to a very important subject. The regulatory value of performance information depends critically on a tolerance for ambiguity and a philosophy that embraces diversity among firms as a source of information rather than an obstacle to overly simplified answers.

# Index

# About the Authors

**Alan R. Beckenstein** is an associate professor of business economics at the Colgate Darden Graduate School of Business Administration of the University of Virginia. He received the A.B. from Lafayette College and the A.M. and Ph.D. from the University of Michigan. He is the coauthor of *The Economics of Multi-Plant Operation: An International Comparisons Study* (Harvard University Press, 1975), and is the author of various articles in economics and management journals on the topics of economics and public regulation. He was formerly a consultant with R. Shriver Associates and served as a consultant to the Department of Energy and a number of private corporations.

**Leslie E. Grayson** is a professor of international business economics at the Colgate Darden Graduate School of Business Administration of the University of Virginia. He received the A.B. from Oberlin College and the A.M. and Ph.D. from the University of Michigan. He is editor of *Economics of Energy* (Darwin Press, 1975), the coauthor of *Management of Public Sector and Nonprofit Organizations,* (Holden-Day, 1980), and the author of *The European National Oil Companies* (John Wiley and Sons, 1980). Formerly he was chief economist of Caltex Oil Corporation (jointly owned by Texaco and Standard of California). His previous academic positions include research associate, Harvard University, Center for International Affairs; adjunct professor economics, Fletcher School of Law and Diplomacy; senior affiliate professor of economics and Ford Foundation Award Scholar, INSEAD, Fontainebleau, France. He has been a consultant to the World Bank, UNCTAD, Departments of Energy and the Interior, Executive Office of the President, and a number of private corporations.

**Susan H. Overholt** is an economic consultant with R. Shriver Associates, Washington, D.C. She received the B.A. from Michigan State University and the M.B.A. from the University of Virginia. She is a former staff assistant to The Nature Conservancy of Arlington, Virginia, as well as a consultant to the Department of Energy and other government agencies.

**Timothy F. Sutherland** is the vice president of public sector consulting for R. Shriver Associates. He received the B.A. from Knox College and the M.B.A. from New York University. He was formerly with the Departments of Energy and Commerce and was project manager for several consulting projects for the Department of Energy.

## DATE DUE